W9-CHI-961

ENCOMIUMS

"With this new novel, Hanshe reinforces his growing reputation as one of today's most original and thought-provoking novelists."

—Keith Ansell-Pearson

"*The Abdication* is an extraordinary mythic delirium-philosophy, rich with erudition and wit, chronicling the exploits of a Heraclitean prophet ushering in nothing less than the Age of Heterology. Long may it unnerve."

—Lance Olsen, author of *Calendar of Regrets*

"Hanshe's phantasmagoric and cunning prose eviscerates accreted mythologies while revealing the tragedy attendant on the death and births of gods. Its controversial premises will enrage and provoke many, but the quality and elegance of the writing will amaze all."

—Nicholas Birns, author of *Theory After Theory*

"*The Abdication* is a visionary novel of dangerous ideas, a theological thriller concerned with the absence of god and the question posed by the phrase: Dionysus versus the Crucified. It is as richly allusive as it is physically direct: a novel of revolt that can at times be revolting in its relentless push to break the mold of idealist thought. As well argued as it is intricately arcane, indeed dense with learning and lore, this book is both experimental and assured, a comedy of high seriousness and gospel of the flesh that our winded civilization has needed for 2,000 years. *Ridendo dicere severum*!"

—Stuart Kendall, author of *Georges Bataille*

Also by Rainer J. Hanshe

The Acolytes

THE ABDICATION

RAINER J. HANSHE

CONTRA MUNDUM PRESS
NEW YORK

Library of Congress Cataloging-in-Publication Data

Hanshe, Rainer J.

The Abdication ❧ Rainer J. Hanshe

—1st Contra Mundum Press ed.

296 pp., 5x8 in.

ISBN 9780983697220

1. A divine comedy. 2. A comedic divinity.

3. Finis metaphysicae. 4. Aeternam risus. 5. ∞

1. Hanshe, Rainer J. 11. Title.

2012934019

THE
ABDICATION

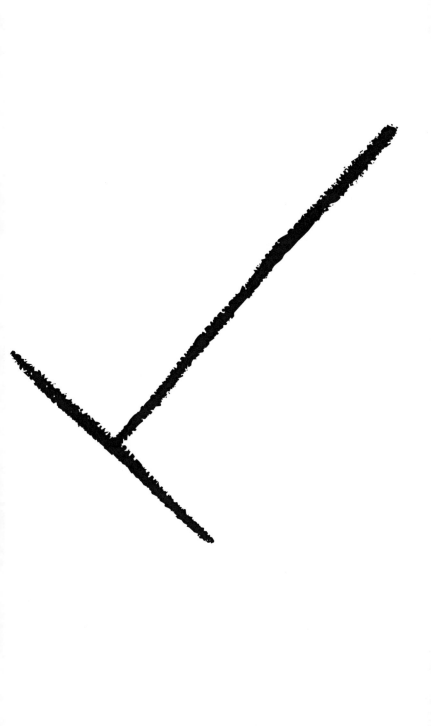

SPRING
2032

ROME

When the kids first began circling Circo Massenzio, it was with a degree of order and harmony, but as they continued circling it, they became more and more disordered, perhaps provoked by the wildly hot, almost violent temperature which, despite the fact that it was just spring, seemed to increase as they played, perhaps provoked by the thrill of their discoveries, or by sheer glee, and due to the disorder, they could not remember when they first began circling Circo Massenzio, so it seemed as if they had never begun circling it, but were always circling and circling it, dust billowing into the air in tiny whorls as they turned to and fro, rocks shooting hither and thither, jettisoned by their tumultuous feet as they scurried here, there, and everywhere, unearthing various treasures, laughter and shouts echoing throughout space as they eventually converged before the remnants that they'd collected during their circling, and picking up piles of them, each of the kids began laying out the eclectic pieces as if they were archeologists, displaying the debris in as ordered a fashion as kids would conceive, all of which happened seemingly spontaneously, as if guided by some inexorable force, and on the ground were displayed grommets and bezels and arbors, cuckoos and pinions and count wheels, chime blocks and bellows and cam-gears, as well as clock-faces of every shape, size, and kind, which they used to line both the outer wall and central island of the Circo, and as they continued laying out the pieces, Circo Massenzio came to resemble a colossal clock graveyard, or the warehouse in which temporality itself was made, or *dissembled* once and for all, for they seemed to have gathered together an endless array of time pieces, though how they ended up in the Circo wasn't

known, but, clearly, thousands upon thousands of clocks from
different eras had been dismantled and scattered there, and
as the kids knelt before their exhibit they began sailing split
washers through the air and rolling escape and drive wheels
across the ground and squeezing suspension springs at one
another while others banged together blocks and weights and
held bells in the air and rang them with hooks and rings and
forks, knocking pendulums into one another as if in and of
themselves they were becoming clocks, and they placed the
cranks and click wheels and double swingers over their bodies
as if the objects were actually organs they required to subsist
and when one of them would collapse from laughter or ex-
haustion, another would take a clock key and turn and turn it
over the heart of the kid until he or she rose from the ground
and began moving again, for even, as such clocks illustrated,
time could come to an end, or so some believed, but it could
begin again from that still point, exploding from nothing into
something, from inertia into *ertia*, and finally they gathered
the last of the pieces, such as verges and bushing and chains, all
of which were brought together in one final frenzied series of
delirious gestures, and as if completing some diabolical puzzle,
micrometers, hex nuts, and commutators were arranged in
some arcane, inexplicable order that to them was very logical
though, clearly, the pieces were not arranged according to any
logic of mechanics, however precise the arrangement was, but,
finally, the mass of hour and minute and second hands were
pinned to the ground with escutcheon and tapered pillars and
pins, with each of the kids giggling as they spun the hands
round and round and round, now in this direction, now in

that, with many of the pillars and pins coming loose and the different hands spinning and spinning into the wildly hot air, sailing here and sailing there, shooting like arrows in countless directions …

As the kids lay on the ground before the detritus and the tumult of the laughter and the dust began to settle, one of them whispered: Now hear! and all listened to the sharp, high, shrill sound of bees just beginning to lead out a storm.

At that moment, the branches of the *ficus* shot forth, its tender shoots appearing and breaking into leaf.

And another kid whispered: Now hear! and in perfect stillness, they hearkened to the coarse, deep bass roaring of the swarm before it began to cluster—the sharp cutting sound of bees calling together their colony.

Thwarp, thwarp, thwarp; thwarp, thwarp, thwarp.

Further along the road, in a field not too far from the Chiesa del Domine Quo Vadis, while awaiting the return of their bandleader, a troupe of musicians were sounding off as goats and monkeys frolicked about them.

And then another kid whispered: Now hear! as the shrill hissing sound of the escort leading the swarm to the woods reached their attentive ears, blending with the roar of the rear part of the swarm, a strange compound only heard from absconding bees.

Thwarp, thwarp, thwarp; thwarp, thwarp, thwarp.

Soon, the *Blastophaga psenes* would come and sacrifice themselves to the fruit of the ficus, losing their wings and almost the entirety of their antennae, dying as the fruit consumes each minuscule corpse, its bruised purple rotundity bursting with death and pleasure.

Thwarp, thwarp, thwarp; thwarp, thwarp, thwarp.

And the animals delighted in the sounds of the inſtruments, which echoed across the field, a cacophony of bells, whistles, drums, and wind instruments of every kind.

Thwarp, thwarp, thwarp; thwarp, thwarp, thwarp.

And numerous men and women of the troupe, coſtumed like satyrs and maenads, danced, vigorously leaping to and fro, ſtraining their bodies to their utmoſt limits, a fluid plaſticity evident in their every kinetic geſture, geſtures often punctuated with ecſtatic yelps.

Turning about, abruptly, the animals tensed up, herding closer together—diſtressed, anxious, excited.

Thwarp, thwarp, thwarp; thwarp, thwarp, thwarp. Thwarp, thwarp, thwarp; thwarp, thwarp, thwarp. Thwarp, thwarp, thwarp; thwarp, thwarp, thwarp.

Suddenly, a helicopter approached from out of the clouds: as it descended, lightning flashes erupted all through the sky and continued to flash and flash from east to weſt, coloring the firmament red, ochre, umber, and blue.

Upon hearing the helicopter approach, the kids grew excited, and when seeing the lightning explode in the sky, they were seized with delight and raced towards the site, their energy completely renewed.

When the bandleader touched ground, in the diſtance, a dense bolt of blue lightning ſtretched from the higheſt cloud in the sky and ſtruck a cypress tree, and then another bolt shot from out of the clouds, this time ſtriking a pine tree, and a third bolt ſtruck, this time shattering perfectly in half a cedar tree, the crack, rumble, and boom of the bolt echoing through

Rome as the trees were felled, bending in every direction, their roots violently torn from the ground with swift velocity.

A piercing trumpet blast erupted as the bandleader, whose face was concealed by a strange, haunting mask, walked from the field to the Appia Antica, accompanied by a cackle of hyenas.

When the kids finally approached and began to gather round the troupe, laughing, the bandleader threw coins to them, tossing the objects in the air, delighting in the sound they made when striking the ground and bouncing to and fro as the kids chased the relics, running about to collect as many of them as they could, even digging between the crevices of the Appia to retrieve the coins that fell between the cracks.

Standing in the middle of the road, the bandleader knelt down on the thick polished cobblestones and, facing north, as if peering directly into the heart of Rome, placed a pestle and mortar before him. Taking a small seed from the pocket of his wide black cloak, he held it aloft, stretching his arms above his head and peering directly into the sky, then placed it in the mortar.

Glancing about, he watched as the troupe drew closer and closer and began to surround him, the animals following in tow, the goats and monkeys edging their way to the inner ring of the circle, the hyenas closing in, accompanied by the kids.

In silence, he held the pestle aloft. Instantly, a deathly quiet pervaded the air—all were transfixed, even the frolicking kids. Gazing at those around him, slowly, he lowered the pestle into the mortar then, gently, *pulverized the seed* ...

Removing another seed from his pocket, he turned southeast, then prostrated himself completely over the mortar and, upon rising, dropped the seed into the bowl; after it settled in the center, gently, he pulverized it, too …

Turning east-southeast, he removed another seed from his pocket, began swaying to and fro like the flame of a candle, then, upon smelling some spices suddenly drift to him through the air, he ceased moving and, in perfect stillness, pulverized the third seed …

Finally, he took a handful of the seeds from his pocket and, one by one, cracked each of them between his fingers, emptying into the mortar the broken remnants, which cascaded from his hand like blackened snowflakes.

Staring into the bowl as if into a vortex or some infinitely contracting horizon, he took the pestle and began turning about, whirling and whirling in a circle, his right palm facing the earth, his left the sky, pivoting on his right foot with perfect agility, each revolution increasing in intensity and velocity. With ceremonial finality, he began chanting, then soon ceased whirling, removed his black cloak, revealing a resplendent burgundy costume, and, kneeling before the mortar, methodically crushed the mass of cracked remnants until they were triturated.

O, bold ones! O searchers, tempters, and experimenters, who of you loves danger? Or to sail upon terrifying seas, venturing into, what—*nothingness?* Are we not those who find riddles intoxicating? Are we not those who delight in questioning, in dissecting, in … *shattering?* But in shattering, are we not seeking—something else? Who can fathom this riddle of the seeds? Who interpret the gestures? Do you not thirst to know? I thirst …

Thwarp, thwarp, thwarp, thwarp, thwarp, thwarp. Thwarp, thwarp, thwarp, thwarp, thwarp, thwarp.

The powdered remains billowed into the air, disappearing with the dust and the wind, swirling away as the helicopter rose and vanished amidst the clouds.

I thirst …

Knocking the mortar, he gently tapped out a rhythm with the pestle that the troupe began to repeat, not only with each percussion instrument, but with their bodies, and the circle began to widen and expand as they varied the rhythms and intensified the force with which they struck their instruments and their bodies, and with each new rhythm members of the troupe would break from the circle and begin dancing frantically, and as more and more of the troupe broke from the circle to dance, each of them moving in a style particular to their body, for the troupe consisted not only of lithe and limber figures, but rotund and malformed ones, he began juggling, casting fiery torches, winnowing-shovels, and wooden blocks, each in the shape of a different diacritical mark or letter, high into the air, and as they marched along the Appia towards Chiesa Quo Vadis, he altered with his juggling the rhythm of the music, and the saxophonists began to breath out sounds, and then the bassoonists, and the trumpeters, and the flank hornists, who summoned everyone onward, the stout, soft, dark sound of their wide conical bores resonating in the air, a sound pleasing to the goats, monkeys, and hyenas.

As the troupe stood before the church and the bandleader continued to juggle, he asked: Is this not the sacred *campus* dedicated to Rediculus, the Roman 'God of the Return'?

One of the troupe shouted: Varro called him Tutanus!

And the twirlers rejoined: We'd like to toot on your anus!

And one of the midgets asked: Isn't it where the famous talking crow is buried?

No! It's the site of a vision!

Balls! It's a vision of nothing, you bozos! Let's march on!

But our journey will be long and hard—should we not make an offering to Rediculus?

Just eat a steak!

Inside there's a marble slab with the imprint of the feet of Jesus!

Is it true? he said, and he threw each of the torches that he was juggling to those before him, and then the winnowing-shovels, which enabled him to juggle the wooden blocks with even greater velocity and variation.

At certain points, it seemed as if some of the blocks almost momentarily h o v e r e d in the air, and to those who watched closely, and whose eyes were keen enough, it was clear that he actually began *to form words* in the air, that he was juggling the blocks in a certain order, that, in fact, *he was forming an entire sentence* with the blocks.

He continued juggling and was amused by the kids attempting to imitate him, tossing as they did each of the coins that they had collected into the air.

The feet … *of Jesus?*

That don't beat Topkapı Palace—they have the beard of Mohammed!

The *whole* beard?

No! Just a piece, but sure as shit it's Mohammed's, and they've got his feet, too, and one of his teeth!

Where's Sappho's clitoris?!

Where's Beelzebub's rectum?!

Where's Jesus's foreskin?!

Where God?

On St. Catherine's finger!

Did they bury it with her?

What? God?

No, the foreskin!

God is the foreskin, and the foreskin is God!

It's not buried; it's in a charred abbey in western France. Charlemagne's golden gift of gifts!

No it ain't—it's in a jail in Calcata.

Not anymore! Thieves stole it from the priest's wardrobe closet!

Is that when the Carmelite nun found it?

She didn't find it; it *appeared* in her mouth and she said it tasted like honey!

If holy prepuces taste like honey, is not honey made of holy prepuces?

Prepuces? Bah! Let's pray to the holy pussy! The immaculate womb of Mary! *Virginitas in partu! Pray-pusses!*

What? Did she birth Him like Zeus birthed Dionysos?

Forget the Holy Grail; let's find the Golden Ring of St.

Caterina!

What about her placenta—did they save that, too?

Yeah, and it's on Mt. Ségur.

No it ain't—it's in the *fundus uteri, inter faeces et urinam*!

What do you want with virgins? Give me sweet, ripened fruit—there is nothing more succulent. Sooner murder an infant in its cradle than nurse unacted desires!

Stopping, the bandleader placed the blocks on the ground and walked towards the entrance of the church.

Hey, where are you going? the revelers enjoined, laughing.

I'm going to Rome to …

Rome? We're in Rome.

I'm going to—*see if my feet are the same size.*

But are you circumcised?!

Turning as if to remove his mask, the bandleader answered: I've been told I taste like honey … but instead of revealing his face, he firmly affixed the mask to his head and turned back.

Let's play on, others shouted, and they continued beating out rhythms, though more and more savage ones, as he walked into the church and the doors closed behind him.

Gathering the torches, the figures in maenad costumes formed a circle with them in the middle of the street; once joined together, the flames of the torches grew hotter and brighter, flickering and snapping in the air as the women approached the church and some of the kids once again tossed their coins into the air, attempting to juggle them while others ran around one another in opposite directions, as if replicating a clock gone haywire, and still others played with the animals.

When at last the doors to the church were opened, the bandleader strode toward the flames, gathered the wooden blocks, and stacked them on top of the torches, at which point they began to burn, prompting him to dance about the torches in a slow, concentrated state, circling them, staring into the conflagration, which his eyes reflected, making it seem as if the fire emerged from his body itself, and as he approached the torches and retrieved the burning blocks, handling them with perfect ease, the fire and his body did, it appeared, begin to blend, so much so that his hands were like flames and the flames were like hands, and the fire, intensifying in degree, was so blistering that the blocks finally disintegrated, and gazing around him, with a gesture, he invited the others to dance, his movements becoming more vigorous, his body twisting and turning with glee as if he had been released from some primordial bond, his body physically articulating his consciousness, as too did the bodies of the women, whose movements became frenzied as the vibrations of the drums and of the other malformed bodies around them coursed through their flesh, their heads snapping back and thrusting forward and side to side as they let down their hair and their shirts slipped from their shoulders, their breasts glistening with sweat, their stomachs expanding and contracting the faster they breathed while others belted animal skins to their waists and brandished serpents, which hissed in the air, their long thin red tongues shooting in and out, almost in tandem with the flames, as if they were but an extension of the conflagration.

Crowning themselves with ivy and oak and smilax in full flower, the women on the periphery of the circle called out to him in unison chanting: Triboulet, Triboulet, lead us on; let's go, let's go, to the center of the city with our songs.

Then paper the city! Let them know, tell one and all, put up posters and hand out bills till the people spill into the streets at your beck and call ... Draw them on! Let us begin!

Crashing cymbals resounded in the air and parade drums boom, boom, boomed.

As his retinue of costumed maenads and corpulent sileni encircled him, Triboulet drew a *salpinx* from the thyrsi with which they danced, and blasting the horn he produced a piercing sound and announced:

Friends! I send you out to gather those of our tribe, the searchers and seekers both bold and brave, the wanderers and nomads, too, go to the farthest ends of the earth and call forth our band—the time has come for us to gather: we alone know what is possible with this troupe!

And so some went forth to gather the infamous brethren as Triboulet commanded, and he continued onward with the remainder of his retinue into the heart of Rome, frolicking along the Appia, releasing people from their homes with the sound of the siss, boom, bang, enticing, seducing, entrancing, drawing one and all on and on as they crossed the Via Cilicia and then the Porta Ardeatina until they reached Parco Scipioni and they circled round and round, the music intensifying with every snaking turn, a burst of drums, cymbals, bells, and double flutes, all commingling into explosive crescendos and points of ecstatic rupture, as if sound itself burst, and

it seemed as if they almost entirely s u s p e n d e d the
rhythms of the music, extending time signatures to points of
near collapse till Triboulet burst into guffaws, at which second
the tempo of the music increased and a raging cacophony commenced, horns screeching, wailing, almost shouting, straining
to cracking points, echoing human cries, animal noises, and
eerie distorted tones, like the sounds of planets spinning at
high velocity, all of which intensified even more when Triboulet blew on two and then three horns simultaneously, sounding certain haunting notes that were signals for tempo changes
and rhythmic shifts, with the cacophony morphing back into
more melodic and mellifluous lines.

Hypnotized by such potent music, all those within its
reach began to dance wildly, and even those not prone to dancing were seized by the music and felt not only stimulated but
that their consciousness began to alter, their perception sharp-
en, with everything around them radiating as if aglow with
nimbuses, and more acute senses of reality were gained as the
sound waves seeped into their pores and entered their muscles
till it felt as if a physical force or warm, steady, powerful fluid
coursed through their bodies, altering their inner stratifications, for the music moved on another plane, a plane where
matter did not exist and everything was interconnected, where
only interrelations of probabilities existed, and new probabilities were what they sought, to penetrate with sound to sub-
atomic levels where continual exchanges of matter and energy,
tongue and brass, human and goat, body and body, sound
and flesh, bone and air, a real exchange of the photons and
electrons of everything around, and as these exchanges were

occurring and each body was transformed just as each thing, element, and more, Triboulet united everyone again and as the flank hornists blew, his retinue continued on and from Via di Porta San Sebastiano they crossed Numa Pompilio Piazza and proceeded up Terme di Caracalla towards Circo Massimo, where they settled and from where numerous members of the troupe went parading forth into the outlying streets of Rome, papering the city, stringing banners here and there, drawing in the piazzas and alleys, marking the streets with chalk and paint, wandering from Monte Aventino to the Colosseum and Monte Esquilino, and from the Quirinale to Salario, Monte Pincio and Piazza del Popolo to Vatican City, with each member of the troupe returning in full regalia, jestering about with magnificent codpieces, bells on their feet, their asses exposed, disrupting the regular affairs of the day, seducing legions of people, embracing the downtrodden and lost, who they cavorted with back towards Circo Massimo across Via Cavour, Via Nazionale, and Viale Trastevere, from Via Conciliazione to Corso Emanuele II, and from Piazza del Popolo down Via del Corso to Piazza Venezia, which they slithered around, splitting into every street, spidering about the Musei Capitolini causing a joyous melee or general tumult, for many were incensed and outraged by the antics of the troupe, especially since scores of them were considered immoral, incivists not suited to a world of prigs and conformists, yet even the puritans felt some strange irresistible sensation whenever hearing the troupe's music.

And, generally, in those they encountered, the troupe produced a sense of overwhelming delight and relief, for the world was beset with famines and earthquakes and nation was warring against nation, which some interpreted as the first birth pangs of a new aeon, for there were many nights when the sun darkened, the moon did not give light, and there were continual meteor showers as if the cosmos itself were at war. Some also thought that a cataclysmic geological shift as devastating as a new lava or ice age was to occur on earth and many around the world were possessed by pervasive and dreadful fears, while several self-proclaimed prophets kept predicting that the end of the world was nigh, though whenever that end neglected to occur and the promised rapture proved not to be, they quickly recalculated their predictions, stated that they'd misconstrued the "signs," and, unabashed, despite the fact that numerous people had committed suicide in fear of the end of the world they'd predicted, heedlessly made renewed prognostications, with no skepticism ever even slightly rupturing their benighted faith. Because of the terrorist attacks that had continued throughout the last two decades, many were beset with disabling paranoia, which, though it abated from time to time, was continually provoked anew through billboards, radio broadcasts, television reports, and announcements on subways and in depots and at airports instructing people to remain constantly vigilant and to beware of suspicious persons and suspicious packages and suspicious actions and to report all such nefarious and threatening suspiciousness to the authorities, for having a "safe day" was a sanctioned imperative, so much so that no one felt free to ruminate or brood or aimlessly loaf about, and tensions between Christians and Muslims had been escalating for the last twenty years and

were recently exacerbated to an unprecedented degree when
the crosses atop both domes of the Church of the Holy Sepulchre in the Old City of Jerusalem were reported as having
been violently knocked from their bases, were nowhere to be
found, and the side of the ceiling of one of the domes was
pierced …

At first, the Israeli government was hesitant to divulge
the extent of the crime, but finally capitulated to international
pressures and the demands of the foreign press, religious organizations, heads of state, and the Papacy and further news
reports revealed that the acts of vandalism were even more
heinous, for not only was every crucifix within the church
missing, but the frescos of the crucifixion had been erased,
and even the ancient graffiti of crosses scratched by medieval
pilgrims on one of the stairwells within the church had been
carved into a maze, while the cross hanging above the altar of
the crucifixion—believed to be the site of Golgotha itself—
had also been violently wrenched from the wall. Catholics of
all persuasions were outraged and staged protests and demon-
strations, decrying the act "an abomination of desolation," with
many calling for vengeance, that is, justice, and others, though
profoundly wounded, for pity and compassion. Although
several extremist Islamic organizations claimed responsibility for the desecration, Israeli police had yet to determine
whether it was, though still exceedingly grievous and morally
offensive, merely the senseless and ignorant act of a band of
"hopelessly degenerate juvenile delinquents" completely devoid
of ethics, or something more dire, a politically or religiously
motivated gesture, possibly the onset of a series of attacks that

might continue and were indicative of a potential religious war. Whatever the case, the world was on tenterhooks—when the dust from the devastation had finally been cleared away, it was discovered that the icon of Christ Pantocrator in the dome of the church had been permanently defaced. The image of the savior's visage had been entirely eliminated and was now nothing but an ashen gray circle which, in its center, contained a large forbidding

In Circo Massimo, the troupe, which had been trailing behind it an enormous ship on wheels, began to unload various items from the vehicle and, much like the kids in Circo Massenzio, display the objects on the ground before them, putting pieces here and there as if haphazardly, ordering them in a way no one could follow or discern, but which possessed to them its own peculiar logic, as if they were agents of chaos, flourishing only in discombobulated states, provoked by such even, inspired by disarray, by frenetic scurrying and pandemonium, though some thought that they were deliberately masking each of their acts, which they engaged in with knowing mischievousness, if not perhaps *metis*. From a rag tag troupe of misfits, musicians, and performers of this stripe, what was one to expect but some form of hijinks and trickery? What they resembled most in their gestures was an orchestra tuning up that, although not wholly discordant, produced the sensation of discord, or something amorphous, an unshaped mass whose many inevitable forms was undetectable but whose energy was mesmerizing, for in the tumult there was nothing staid or ossified, only desire or force in motion, a sense of searching, aimless play, and freedom, an escalating, excited tension of *something* on the verge. And all of the people that the troupe gathered and led to Circo Massimo congregated around it, watching as various members of the troupe began assembling different structures and others enthralled the crowd with musical performances and acrobatic acts.

When seeing the placement of the numerous triangular structures throughout the field, the kids realized that the troupe was constructing enormous swing sets, and when the chains were strung to the overhead poles and the leather seats at last affixed, the kids streamed wildly into the arena exclaiming and exulting, many of them shouting what sounded like A-OH! A-OH! A-OH! and something to the effect of *Pix*! but their almost violent utterances were considered mere gibberish, the sheer delight of kids playing with words and letters as if they were nothing but sounds to be rolled upon the tongue with orbicular pleasure, which is all the sounds may have been, gibberish, but the musicians listened attentively to their aural ejaculations and several of them picked up their utterances and began chanting them as the kids leapt into the swings and were being rocked back and forth, delighting in the sensation of hovering in mid-air in a kind of euphoria, approaching the sky with each forward arc, feeling as if they could seize the sun or the moon with each oscillation, and as they continued swinging, they developed a rhythm with the musicians, with

everyone chanting A on the upswing and OH! on the down-
swing, and after three full oscillations they all shouted: PIX!
the word bursting from their mouths, the X extending into
a long, protracted sssssssssssssssssssssss that sounded
like rain issuing from their lips and which culminated in
monstrous giggling, and when the cackling frenzy dissipated,
they began chanting in unison again:

A--------OH!

A--------OH!

A--------OH!

PIXsssssssssssssssssssssssssssssssssssssssssssssss!
till even the adults on the sidelines began to join in the chanting, provoked by the musicians, who wandered through the
crowd, prodding them with gestures and taunts and aural
commands to involve them directly in the festivities until there
was no longer any clearly demarcated boundary between the
troupe and the crowd.

As the chants resounded in the air, echoing it was later
reported to the Colosseum and even across the Tevere, at the
southern end of Circo Massimo, other members of the troupe
were constructing a strange nine meter high single swing
whose arms were not made of chains or rope but steel, and ivy
and garlands were wound about the structure, and sitting atop
the columns were birds about to take flight. When the troupe
finished assembling it, Triboulet mounted the swing in silence
and began to gather momentum by squatting and standing
up, the swing oscillating higher and higher in each direction.
Never having seen such a swing before, not even being able
to recollect such a swing existing in ancient Rome, or even

amongst the intrepid Minoans, those present found the object both intriguing and fascinating if not, because of its extreme height, dangerous, and they watched Triboulet with awe, alarm, and trepidation, wondering how far he would swing in either direction, and, if he went too far, if he would fall from such a height, for the object seemed designed to enable one to circle the swing completely. While on their swings the kids remained bound within one domain, never truly leaving the terrestrial realm, Triboulet seemed on the verge of vaulting into the celestial realm, or of *uniting* the terrestrial and the celestial realms—he did not believe that they were actually separate—through his swinging, and the anticipation mounted as he thrust himself further and further in either direction, soaring backwards and forwards, perfectly poised, every now and then emitting a deep guttural grunt, like a samurai harnessing *chi*. As he continued to swing, the midgets of the troupe were decanting from giant beehive shaped barrels that they'd wheeled into the Circo a light golden liquid into clay flagons, and after filling each flagon, the midgets would distribute them throughout the crowd, partaking themselves and encouraging others to consume the nectar, a gently sparkling drink neither dry or sweet made of fermented thyme honey, quinces, and water sunned for forty days at the time of the early rising of Sirius, a star Triboulet revered.

Console yourselves in your distresses! Drink fresh if you can come by it!

First with melikratos, *then with sweet wine*!

And so the flagons were passed around, with everyone imbibing the refreshing drink, consuming it as they watched

Triboulet continue to swing, and the more of the nectar that
they drank, the more they chanted Triboulet on, for they admired such daring and longed to witness impossible feats, and
challenging the very force of gravity, Triboulet at laſt swung
beyond the normal oscillating point of the arc of a swing and
made a full 180° turn, soaring from one direction to the other,
completing an entire half-circle, then soaring backwards 220°
and as he projected himself forward again, squatting and
ſtanding with greater ſpeed and force, at laſt, he swung
completely over the ſpindle of the swing and, momentarily,
h o v e r e d directly above the top of it as if gravity itself
were suſpended ~ it produced a sense of weightlessness: and
as he hovered there, ſtill as a hummingbird, *everyone* seemed
to hover with him, to at leaſt *feel* as if they were hovering between one realm and another, as if they had somehow sur-
mounted the ground, then, swiftly: — he soared backwards
again until jettisoning himself forward with prodigious
velocity, completing a full 360° turn, swinging and swinging round the ſpindle several times, uniting earth and sky in
one fluid continuous motion, prompting everyone to exult in
Triboulet's feat, chanting:

A--------Oн!
A--------Oн!
A--------Oн!

PIXsssssssssssssssssssssssssssssssssssssssssss!
When Triboulet dismounted the swing, he seized a megaphone from the ship-car and declaimed through it, inviting
the crowd to join the troupe on the field and to participate in
the swinging, for aside from the smaller swings the troupe had

erected for the kids, there were larger swings of various types for adults to swing in, too, and so as the troupe carnied around Circo Massimo crashing cymbals, booming parade drums, and sounding off with trombones and trumpets and instruments of every kind, the spectators playfully jostled their way to the swings and rocked back and forth, swinging one another with great pleasure, but while several people attempted to mount Triboulet's swing, no one could span an arc even half that of his arcs, nor swing for more than two minutes, and peering at them through his haunting mask, he blew upon his *salpinx* and released himself into the fray and a general euphoria suffused everyone in the Circo, and as that state of becoming overtook them, that which originally isolated each of them from one another began to dissipate and instead of being like disparate, isolated stars in the cosmos, they felt like integral elements of a constellation, if not like dust in the cosmos, and that they were not separate either from the goats, monkeys, and hyenas that surrounded and wandered amongst them, but were all of a piece, folded together like entrails, though the animals may even have been of a higher plateau, and they expressed themselves not through speech but through gestures, and as they danced, their movements conveyed enchantment, their limbs fluid, graceful, rhythmic, uncanny sounds emanating from them as they exulted in their euphoria, night engulfing the culmination of day and turning towards the future.

In the midst of the darkness, Triboulet led several of the women to the southern end of Circo Massimo and kneeling before the tower, he took a goat by the front legs, lifted it into the air, and kissed it, after which the women seized the animal and brought it to the ground, firmly holding it in place and softly caressing its body to instill in it a degree of calmness; then, in one expeditious gesture, the goat was beheaded: — when its stately head fell to the earth, Triboulet lifted it by the horns and gazed into its eerie face as the women continued to hold the body of the animal, which trembled and convulsed in their hands, the viscous fluids gushing out into a bowl they had placed beneath it, the organs straining to emerge from the severed neck as if it were a womb. Once it ceased twitching, the women held the goat aloft and Triboulet slowly cut its belly open, then tore away the skin to divest the beast of its organs, which were collected in another bowl. Removing the entrails from the vessel, Triboulet gently placed them on the ground and by torchlight, stared at them, studying them under the flames, examining the folds, color, and texture, and he began envisioning something as he meditated on the turns within the coils of the intestines—gazing back at the stately head of the goat, he was transfixed by its hieratic smile as the women cleaned the animal and then, after beheading several others, began cooking them to end their acts with a feast.

The next day, the troupe began gathering masses of imperial porphyry and transporting it to Circo Massimo and Villa Pamphili. There was such an abundant volume of the igneous purple rock that it was startling, and the continuous conveyance of it was almost more of a spectacle than the troupe's customary parading through the streets, perhaps due in part to the fact that no one expected such a rag tag band of musicians, jongleurs, and acrobats—or whatever it was they were—to engage in such laborious activities, but they seemed

to thrive on difficult tasks and exhibited the resilience and re-
sourcefulness of pioneers forging entirely new terrain, which
gained them the respect of the more orthodox Romans, who
found their regular antics unsettling if not immoral. When
questioned who they were and where they hailed from, they
rejoined that they were just strangers and pilgrims, wandering here and there as impulse saw fit, guided by their instincts,
propelled it almost seemed by the wind, or some unarticulated
aim discerned by Triboulet. What was most impressive was
when they began assembling large portions of the porphyry
in Circo Massimo into some jagged incomprehensible mass,
lifting through a system of pulleys and winches one piece of
the rock on top of another till it resembled some monumental misshapen blob, the plagioclase crystals glistening in the
spring sun, the rock's dark purple hue a stark contrast to the
blasted dirt and trampled grass of the arena. As they continued to construct the mass, it was found even more astonishing,
for over time it grew in height to 160 meters, which made some
wonder if they were building a new Tower of Babel, a view rejected by the Vatican and other religious authorities but which
many of the public retained for several weeks, hoping in fact
that, as with that ancient structure, this one too would meet
its doom, for more than being incensed by an ambitious and
grandiose act, many people were unsettled by the structure
because they found it enigmatic, incomprehensible, a monument to absurdity all too characteristic of the senseless, bland,
academic art that dominated the latter half of the twentieth
century, the con-art of conceptualizations that could never be
animated into form but only theorized in explanatory placards

placed adjacent to a work as if it were a cripple yearning for
a crutch. Although many expected the troupe to construct
something absurd if not outrageous, no one reckoned that they
would have spent so considerable an amount of time devoted
to building an entity that insipid and jejune. But their efforts
were only just beginning, and what many finally realized was
that they were not building a Babelean Tower let alone sculpting—if one could even refer to such a collocation of material as
sculpting—some arid monument to mediocrity before which
fatigued cynics could stand in plain awe, worshipping ordinari-
ness, interpreting it as sublime so as to feel as if the monumental is actually within their grasp. No. Like those of a medieval
guild, the members of the troupe were slowly, anonymously,
carefully giving form to something, were not merely collocat-
ing material, but actually shaping it, molding it, giving it definition, patiently birthing something that, eventually, would be
completely animated, would that is be given dynamic arresting life, like a species evolving, mercilessly shedding its primitive, archaic layers in its struggle to become what it is, in its
drive for futurity, to destroy all that retards its continuous and
often necessarily violent transformation. One sensed in their
devotion to the sculpture the burgeoning of something terrible, something tremendous, if not perhaps even cataclysmic,
as if the truly new were on the verge, ready to burst forth from
the rock, to split reality into pieces or rather, to obliterate a
millennium of obfuscating encrustations as they were pitch-
ing the rock with their chisels and mallets and roughing out
the general shape of the sculpture, which remained beyond
everyone's discernment yet was still utterly bewitching.

And in the midst of this revelation, as the monumental purple edifice was emerging into an early stage of its destined form, news flashes hurriedly reported that, unbeknownst to the local residents of Kent, England, and to the Archbishop of the church, who was elsewhere at the time, Canterbury Cathedral had been completely covered in thin folds of black polyamide "in the dead of night." The unknown perpetrators of the bizarre act, which locals found perplexing if not incendiary, were unfortunately aided the police said by the entirety of the county of Kent having suffered from an unexpected blackout. When the prank was reported, power had still yet to be restored. Once the fire department finally arrived and attempted to remove the fabric, the firefighters were jolted by high levels of static electricity, and when rippled by a small breeze, electrical charges continued to emerge from the fabric as it billowed, undulating against the building, popping and crackling in a frenetic dance, the jolts streaming around the old edifice like elongated electric snakes, actually searing parts of the fabric and, as was soon realized, much of the building, too, making it seem like thin black snakes wound themselves around the entire structure as if to strangle it. Once finally neutralized, the firemen began to unravel the fabric, and as they were removing it from the building and more and more bystanders began to gather round, gazing at the seemingly innocuous but beguiling spectacle both with awe and trepidation and not sure whether to admire or fear it, one of them noticed that, when held at a certain angle and the sun streamed through the fabric and made it shimmer, the material appeared to contain rows and rows of script. Under closer examination,

the fabric it was revealed resembled a patchwork of sewn together broadsheets, not actual broadsheets, but a simulacrum
of hundreds and hundreds of 18th century style broadsheets;
however, no one at the site could decipher the script, nor did
they know what language it was written in, but it was presumed by the police to be "something ancient." Soon, it was
discovered that an even more disconcerting and mysterious
event had occurred—as layer upon layer of fabric was unwound from the cathedral, everyone present was terribly
alarmed by the strange occurrence that, at 8:00 AM, Kent was
silent. Bell Harry, the oldest bell in the church, normally rung
every morning at exactly 8:00 AM to signal the opening of the
church, did not sound. It was the first time since the 12th century that such a silence pervaded Kent: — the deathly quiet
was in and of itself terrifying, a haunting, inhuman silence,
bringing even atheists, agnostics, and the lukewarm apathetic
horde to the scene of the crime. After the fabric was at last
removed and the Archbishop and the police finally entered
the cathedral, they discovered to their disbelief that not only
was Bell Harry gone, but that every single one of the 21 bells of
Canterbury Cathedral were "missing." Oxford Tower, Arundel
Tower, and Angel Steeple, commonly known as the Bell Harry
Tower, were, astoundingly, all somehow divested of their bells,
which ranged in weight from nearly two to three and a half
tons each. Once the news reached those outside, a vagrant
turned to the crowd and, laughing, regaled them with a tale,
proclaiming that, "while all ye were sleepin' I saw the culprits,
O yes, true fable true, and them great bells were hanging from
a mares neck, 'tis right as day is night, but it was loaded with

brie and fresh herring and sausages, too, and I canted away for
I wanted some of that hoggish stuff, beleeve for a truth, for I
saw where they gathered together, sulfured, hopurymated,
moiled and bepist," and he started micturating, unleashing a
flood at their feet, proclaiming he "just wanted to share with
you my wine, but only in sport, for there's nuthin' like drawing
out your *mentul* into the open aire," and he was quickly shut-
tled away, though his unruly laughter echoed through the
crowd, and his last peculiar words hung in the air like circling
crows: It was Aesma-Daeva, good ol' Modo-Mahu you right
attenuated asses! Dem bells dangled from 'is mare and 'is hair!"
but no one knew what in the name of Christ he was talking
about. As press releases instantaneously shot around the
world, it was recounted that Dunstan, Mary, Crundale, Elphy,
Thomas, and Jesus were all missing, though not the original
Jesus, which led to bizarre and comical inquiries because some
believers around the world actually thought that it was being
reported that Jesus himself—Himself—had returned but it
was not the original Jesus but another Jesus and they were
perplexed first by how it was possible for Jesus to get lost and
second by how it was possible to determine whether Jesus was
actually Jesus and not another Jesus yet, since there was only
one Jesus, anyone claiming to be Jesus that wasn't Jesus was
clearly not Jesus, though the Mexicans did make that confusing, and others argued that since Jesus was the incarnation of
God that what must have happened was that both God and
Jesus had returned at the same time and when seeing God
some people thought He was Jesus and when seeing Jesus
some people thought He was God, while others couldn't tell

them apart, and then complicated theological discussions ensued as to how it would be possible to distinguish between
God and Jesus if both returned at the same time and, if it took
2000 years for him—Him—to return, which was unlikely
since he promised that "his generation" would live "to see it
all," meaning those of his time would witness the very passing
away of heaven and earth, but just to hypothesize, if he did
return, would he look older (did he age in the interim between
leaving and returning, or did he remain perpetually 33 as Mary
remained perpetually intact, both vaginally and—of course—
anally?), would he still have a beard and the same clothes, or
would he be in modern dress, though still have the crown of
thorns, stigmata, etc., a confusion that arose simply because
the news reports neglected to include the important detail
that Dunstan, Mary & alia were not actually "missing persons,"
abducted employees that is of the cathedral, but bells, the
names of but some of the missing bells of Canterbury Cathedral and that the original Jesus was not actually missing for
the original Jesus—the bell—was destroyed in an earthquake
when the campanile of the cathedral fell and the Jesus that was
rehung was not in fact the same Jesus of course but another
Jesus entirely, although some still referred to it as Jesus, despite
the fact that there is not two Jesuses, just one, though in the
age of the *Überdoppelt*, few seemed to be concerned with the
value of originals and were perfectly satisfied with near-exact
replicas and thus wouldn't mind a virtual savior, too. Aside
from discovering the enigma of the missing bells, initial local
reports also stated that the dean, canons, and other employees
of the cathedral were all dead, with journalists speculating

upon the motive for their possible murder, and hints of some anti-Catholic conspiracy began to arise and spread like a contagion. The employees though were not dead but, doctors diagnosed, in deep catatonic stupors which, it was predicted, they would eventually waken from, at which point the police hoped to be able to gain much needed information about what had happened the night of the crime. In the midst of the outrage, confusion, and perplexity, the police first thought the strange incident to be an art school prank, or a group of eco-terrorists imitating the work of a long-forgotten and insignificant "environmental artist" as a statement and act of homage, but the stunt was, they believed, too elaborate and complicated for mere art students to "pull off," whereas it seemed far too uncharacteristic to be the act of eco-terrorists, who, they didn't think, would use the simulacra of broadsheets to make a statement since they were far more overt and prone to obsessively composing all of their proclamations in Helvetica, so the actual culprits remained unidentified. Although nothing in the church was physically destroyed, the incident brought to mind the recent vandalism in Israel and while various authorities speculated as to who the possible culprits were, everyone from the members of England's black magic sects to terrorists, radical protestant reformers, and the acolytes of the newly revived Abbey of Thelema all claimed responsibility for the event. As police began to investigate further, linguists were enlisted to decipher the strange script embedded in the fabric which, at last, was reported to be an ancient form of Aramaic, thus definitively ruling out the art students and eco-terrorists as possible suspects. Although the linguists could discern the script was Aramaic, they were not able to actually read it, thereby further delaying the resolution of the riddle, which would only be solved once the Aramaic scholars that were newly summoned arrived, or so they presumed. Over the course of the ensuing days, as more facts were being unveiled, county officials declared that there was not in fact an "organic power outage" but that the incident was actually a load shedding or "rolling blackout" and that, most probably, whoever was behind the theft of the bells also intentionally engineered the power outage in order to facilitate their crime. When electricity was at last restored, the Archbishop went to the Norman crypt to meditate upon the disturbing affairs and saw to his consternation that the statue of St. Augustine, the first Archbishop of Canterbury, was hanging by his feet from one of the high arches in the east end of the crypt.

With the occurrence of such worrying events, it was no wonder that Triboulet and his troupe were welcome relief from the unsettling inexplicabilities besieging the world, events to which few people knew how to respond, except, generally, with outright rage, but outbursts of that sort proved to be indicative of nothing but impotence. Laughter, Triboulet thought, was the powerful and liberating response. Yet no one in Circo Massimo was thinking of such affairs and after admiring the initial genesis of the troupe's monumental sculpture and relishing the perplexity it provoked, unbeknownst to all, Triboulet left the scene to climb Arco di Giano. When he reached the top of the arc, he spread several goat skins on the ground, then laid down on the animal bedding, remaining completely still. In that motionless, silent state of becoming, he hearkened to the reverberations within his body and while gazing into the sky, felt vast dimensions of time streaming into his nerves and the tumult of world history was projected before him like a kaleidoscope unfolding, its phantasmagoric pictures shooting outward into crystalline forms, then collapsing in upon themselves, the visions contracting and expanding like a palpitating heart, each ventricle violently throbbing, pulsating, breathing with life and death, or contracting and expanding like a concertina organ, endlessly elongating as if it were being stretched into infinity, slowly, perilously, but then instantly collapsing and with inevitable force, or like a dense fresco whose layers never seemed to end, with each erased layer creating a palimpsest for the previous layer, though the residue of every preceding layer was always there, even if only as a faint, spectral trace, yet several images were more than just spectral traces and when the visage of Aristarchus and the town of Frauenburg struggled to merge before him, the images trembling like crevices colliding together, he suffered an apoplectic fit and while in a state of seeming paralysis, time seemed like nothing but an ever diminishing fold of phyllo dough, yet as it crumbled in his hands while he twitched and trembled, his body contorting this way and that, time transformed into a bullet, but traveling in reverse, and Triboulet watched as he saw the species itself in reverse, and as it devolved from *homo sapiens* to *homo neanderthalensis* to *homo rhodesiensis* and beyond, as it was in a sense vanishing, though not back to dust, he was witnessing its actual evolution, just as he began to witness in reverse the geological history of the earth and its formation, from the seemingly static continents

and the rising of world sea levels, he saw before him the linking of South and North America, the cooling cycle and the
exposure of the land bridge between Alaska and Asia to the
monumental rise of the Andes, the southward extension of
the Meso-American peninsula and the uplift of mountains
in the western Mediterranean and he thought: *In principio?*
and his vision continued with the rising of the Alps in Europe through the African plate forcefully straining north into
the Eurasian plate, *and so it was* to the mixture of equatorial
currents with Antarctic waters, Australia's splitting from the
southern continent, and the vanishing of the Tethys, yet he
did not see anyone or anything hovering over the surface of
the water, but the continued splitting of Gondwana and Africa's migration toward Europe, India's to Asia, and the tectonic
collision and formation of the majestic Himalayas and the
Mediterranean Sea, *and so it was* to the cracking of Pangaea
into the present-day continents, the widening of the Atlantic
Ocean, the first onset of the orogenies, Gondwana's breaking
into South America, Antarctica, and Australia as well as the
formation of the South Atlantic and Indian Oceans yet, even
there he did not see anyone or anything hovering over the surface of the water, but he did witness the magnificent undersea
mountain chains lifting along the welts and raising eustatic
sea levels worldwide, with seas narrowing and advancing and
receding, leaving thick marine deposits squashed between coal
beds, but he did not see any vast waste, let alone some darkness covering the deep; instead, he watched the biodiversity of
oceans increasing as they became more saturated just as rich
marine fossils and terrestrial fauna formed and massive lava

beds were laid down, leading to the formation of the sublime Deccan Traps, *and so it was* to the Gulf of Mexico opening a new rift between North America and the Yucatan to the concentration of nearly all of the earth's land mass into the single supercontinent Pangaea, which was not the result of merely letting something be but some actual tumult, *and so it was* to tectonic deformation and the dramatic rifting of Pangaea to the flourishing of lush coal swamps around the northernmost glaciers, major marine extinction and active mountain building as Gondwana collided with Laurussia resulting in the Hercynian and Alleghenian orogeny and the extension of the newly uplifted Appalachian Mountains southwestward as the Eurasian plate welded itself to Europe along the line of the Ural Mountains, *and so it was* to the end of stable greenhouse conditions and the formation of ice caps on Gondwana, which drifted over the south pole, but it was not possible to say whether it was good or not, it just was, *and so it was* to the formation of the Cambrian continents resulting from the breakup of the Neoproterozoic supercontinent Pannotia to the laying down of strata in epicontinental seas, massive, rapid continental accretion, supercontinent cycles, orogenic activity, and glaciations to the heavy metamorphosis of rocks into deep-water sediments, such as graywackes, mudstones, volcanic sediments, and banded iron formations, with the earth's crust cooling and continental plates beginning to form along with the establishing of the magnetic field to the formation of the Solar System, the large clouds of gas and dust around the sun, all of which Triboulet did not find good or bad but necessary and inevitable, for destruction begat creation endlessly —

non fuit initium, and so it was: the earth stretching backwards billions of years to its very absolute seeming beginning until the explosion occurred and everything dwindled to a single small point and then expanded, as if the explosion was not strictly a beginning, but an end as well, and an infinite cycle of cosmic aeons were revealed to him, and returning through time, he recognized anew the devastating turns humanity had taken, in particular, the one devastating turn, an immobilizing, dangerous gesture rooting it to its archaic, primitive past, crippling it, a time which pivoted around ... but a new pathway was in sight, and as he witnessed the different ages of the earth erupting before him, he heard the sound of gates opening, of the world on the brink, as if the folds of time were unraveling, generating a sound like scores of atom bombs going off in succession and echoing through the cosmos: — it was a prelude to a philosophy of the future.

Rising from the ground, he removed his mask and surveyed all of Rome, gazing in each cardinal direction, then pivoting on his right foot, he spun and spun in a circle, moving in one direction, then another until—stopping, he whispered something into the wind, gesturing as if to history itself, and then firmly affixed the mask to his face. Lifting a *salpinx* to his lips, he made a long piercing note with the instrument, then climbed down the arc and walked over Ponte Palatino into Trastevere, gathering outcasts and roustabouts and all manner of people as he wandered along, meandering eventually to the Janiculum—from there, he gazed back towards Arco Giano and saw the open gates ...

Continuing on, Triboulet entered Villa Doria Pamphili

and as the troupe progressed with roughing out the shape of
their monumental sculpture in Circo Massimo, he assessed
the locale of the park. Gazing at the landscape, he imagined
how he would structure the field and saw animated before his
eyes the very work that he would construct just northeast of
the lake. Since it would require an oval expanse one hundred
and twenty by two hundred feet across, he began clearing the
ground with other members of the troupe, hacking down and
deracinating every tree obstructing the area, leveling the earth
to prepare for his gift.

After burning one of the deracinated trees and scatter-
ing its ashes on the ground where his gift would be formed,
the shaping of the porphyry commenced, and the sound of it
being hewn into large rough blocks echoed throughout Villa
Pamphili. Normally, the goats, monkeys, and hyenas frolicked
around Triboulet wherever he was, but the noise disturbed the
animals and they roamed to other parts of the park, often accompanied by the kids, who became their persistent compan-
ions, with many wondering if they were not actually animals
of some kind, too, for there was something distinctly inhuman
about them. From the size and sheer volume of the blocks,
many reckoned that Triboulet was going to build a temple
of some kind, though to what no one knew, and persistent
inquiries were humorously deflected as the stones were piled
at different points around the perimeter of the oval which he
marked out only with gestures.

As those gathered at the park observed Triboulet's actions, the work resembled to them simply that of a construction site and they were bemused, for they expected something

far more spectacular, or strange, from him. At very least, they longed for something as monumental as what was being constructed in Circo Massimo, even if they didn't understand it but, in fact, when he finally began to construct what he envisioned, it was evident that he was only building walls with the porphyry blocks, which many found pedestrian while others sensed that he was not just making some common quotidian edifice, but something more mysterious, something perhaps — mythic. And although the monument in Circo Massimo had still yet to receive any clear definition, it was thought that, together, the structures would form some kind of riddle, or that they were not mutually exclusive and each would clarify the other, offer insight into the nature or meaning of both.

Slowly, patiently, Triboulet worked in silence, concentrated as if upon some fateful task, unperturbed by the expectations of those around him, and in several hours he completed the first long stone wall, which stood eight feet high and marked the onset of his vision.

Although those observing him found the wall well-constructed and, perhaps, impressive for its size, essentially it was nothing more to them than a straight wall that ended in a slight curve. If anything, it resembled a post-modern site-specific sculpture, what many would find an affront to classical aesthetics, if not humanity itself.

Standing before it, Triboulet remained silent, then slowly paced around it in a state of deep concentration, gently gliding his hand against the wall as if feeling some force, or the pressure of gravity, and wandering away from it, he walked to a point diagonally across from the beginning of the wall, and, pacing there, measured out the next segment.

Taking a large block from one of the piles, Triboulet placed it on the ground as if laying a foundation ſtone and then began carrying more and more blocks over; although the same height as the other wall, this one was quite short, and, in its bluntness, evoked rapidity.

After finishing it, Triboulet built a number of similar short walls at different points throughout the area, none of which however made clear what he was conſtructing, though some thought that he was building giant ſtone words and that, eventually, what he was ſpelling out would be made apparent, while ſtill others thought it merely some confused corral for his animals, or a prison for the unruly kids.

As days and weeks passed and they ſtruggled to decipher the edifices, he continued to build a series of other relatively ſtraight walls at irregular points around the ſpace in which he was concentrated, thus generating in those observing his acts, as did the indeterminate edifice in Circo Massimo, a similar sense of perplexity.

It was however when he began to build a series of lengthy curved walls, all of which were at odds with the immediate if not greater environment, a division of it wherein the walls began to declare their own area and were not an embellishment or decoration of the exiſting ſpace, let alone the buildings within it, that a greater sense of ſpecificity was beginning to at laſt emerge. The diſtance between some of the walls was not the same, but decreased towards two central points, which resembled hollows or caverns, while the walls reaching those same points were also greater in height than those further away from them.

In gazing at what he had constructed so far, some pondered that what in fact he was building was a stone simulacrum of entrails, though they didn't use either word, and as those at the site studied the complex edifice, they concurred that it did actually resemble "guts" as they said, yet their recognizing such a pattern did not please but only perplex them further as innards did not seem to them a fitting subject for art, or whatever it was that Triboulet was making. He continued with his work though and, after a month, suddenly, when he began to connect some of the existing curving walls, block others off, and create passageways between some, at last they realized that he was building a labyrinth, but it was peculiar, quite different from any other labyrinths they had ever seen. Unlike the round, unicursal mazes typically found in cathedrals, this labyrinth was oval in shape and organic rather than rigidly formal or heraldic. Its path changes could not be found on the axis between the entrance and the center but were more ruthless, embodying elements of chance and necessity, of danger, with the risk of continual error and its attendant angst. Instead of one central chamber, it contained two, but there was no central axis between the entrance and the two chambers, since the labyrinth was multicursal, yet its central chambers did preserve an equilibrium, as if between two different forces, and the labyrinth contained seven turns or decision points, where the path choice could compound error upon error, with each path changing direction in a seemingly random fashion, leading to the possible repeated retracing of one's steps, of a nearly endless series of turning and turning and turning, leading here, there, to twists, turns, *cul-de-sacs.*

As people pondered the maze, wondering why it was built, why this kind of maze in particular was made, did it signify something, or was it just an amusement, and more, the truly anxious question of what if anything was in each of the central chambers, Triboulet constructed the final surrounding wall, the wall that closed in the entire labyrinth, save for the foreboding entrance, and then built a doorway, sealing the passageway to the labyrinth so that it could not be entered or exited.

Once the final porphyry block was cemented in place, as Triboulet circled the labyrinth in silence, the hyenas returned, and the kids quickly followed suite: — in the midst of their laughter, he searched and searched for fertile soil in which to plant something to commemorate the construction of the labyrinth. As they wandered throughout Villa Pamphili, they came upon a dying mustard tree and, full of avid glee, the kids knelt before it and with absolute delight, began snapping its broken branches in pieces, pulling what of it they could to the ground and tearing its roots out, most of which had begun to rot, making the soft, damp wood come apart in their hands like weakened connective tissue—when the hyenas grabbed the roots from their hands, it pulled apart as easily as tender pork, but they quickly spat the remnants from their mouths as if they were contaminated. While the kids continued removing the roots, Triboulet dug out the base of the tree; once the area was fully excavated, he turned the soil over till it was a rich dark black and then planted scores of *Corallorhiza maculata*, or spotted coralroot, a red, fleshy, sensual orchid that he admired because it resembled female genitalia and made him think of Baubo. Standing before the newly planted seeds, he remained in a state of deep concentration, thinking of the majesty of those seed capsules, of how one seed capsule from a single flower could contain up to four million seeds and he dreamt of their dispersing into the air like minute dust particles or single-celled spores and wondered what they would give birth to. In the midst of his meditation, a radio broadcast echoed through the park announcing that a strange sign had been mounted on the Bab Tuma gate in Damascus:

AΩ

Ceci n'est pas un Christ

SUNDAY
MAY 16
2032

The unpredictable and astonishing arrival in Rome of Triboulet and his troupe was likened by many to the arrival of a
cult, for although they seemed to have no precepts, preached
nothing, did not seek obedient and undoubting acolytes, and
were, it was held, merely but some cross between a circus and
a marching band, they exerted upon many a considerable degree of attraction, if not unreserved fascination, and people
flocked to them with attendant zeal. It may simply have been
out of necessity though, not religious fervor, though many
were driven by such impulses, for in the midst of the apocalyptic atmosphere that besieged the epoch, there was a pervasive
desire if not urgent need for strong relief, which people found
in the company of Triboulet and his troupe, though it was
doubtful that even few of them laughed as he laughed—in his
laughter there was something uncanny, a chilling and superior
strength: — it was a laughter born not of forgetting, let alone
of simple ridicule or impotent, disaffected post-modern irony,
but of indomitable and fearless lucidity, of a direct confronta-
tion with that which is most terrifying and questionable, of a
dogged encounter with abysses. Once, he was heard to ask:
Who among you can laugh and be uplifted at the same time?
Whoever climbs the highest mountains and laughs about all
tragic plays and tragic wakes. Are you strong enough to laugh
at what is tragic?

Such cryptic remarks made him akin to a prophet of
some kind, or a modern sage, but one completely devoid of
pity and of any comforting, conciliatory ethics, and it always
seemed as if there was something he was concealing, that his
actual identity, if one could speak of such, was not apparent

and that the full revelation of his being, if that was possible to witness, would be deeply unsettling, and not simply because he might have been a hermaphrodite as some conjectured. If he was not actually the leader of a cult, what however began to alarm many politicians, as well as the Papacy, was that Triboulet and his troupe seemed to possess some irresistible magnetic power that prompted people to abandon whatever they were doing to participate in their activities. It had been eons since an enigmatic figure of Triboulet's kind exerted such hypnotic allure over so many people; it was so peculiar and atypical it seemed like the fervent happening of an early century. And it was not only younger, careless, or radical sects of people that were lured by the troupe, but all strata of individuals, for even managers, chief executives, and vice presidents abandoned their work when hearing the troupe's music, only to return to their positions, sometimes days if not weeks later, completely bemused, something in them having significantly altered. Although the troupe did seek to provoke such events, Triboulet himself was disturbed when he discovered that the day and time of his arrival was being hailed as a propitious if not prophetic sign. After learning from members of his troupe that the trees which were felled by the bolts of lightning when he landed on the Appia Antica were being revered as sacred relics, the objects were retrieved and brought to Circo Massimo for the feast the troupe was to stage.

That evening, after hanging long, luxurious crushed red velvet banners in Circo Massimo and Villa Pamphili, the troupe distributed belladonna, henbane, and sunflowers throughout

both places, yet the most magnificent display was an altar at
the head of Circo Massimo which contained not only resplendent arrangements of those flowers, but also a profusion of ivy,
moly, and mandragora, all of which overflowed from the table
and cascaded onto the ground as if spreading out of control.
After preparing for their feast, Triboulet and his troupe, all of
whom were dressed in scarlet vestments, jestered through the
streets of Rome, each of them snaking through different quarters of the city, piping on double flutes, the haunting, eerie
music of the instruments resounding in the air, which when
everyone played together resembled the sound of a mighty
wind. And as they meandered through the various parts of
the city, frolicking about with animal glee, they gave flutes to
whomever joined them, and when the instruments were all
sounded together, the choral effect of the music resembled an
even greater mighty wind, one never in fact ever heard before,
for this was a truly new wind. And when those that the troupe
gathered all finally converged at Circo Massimo, the sound intensified to such a degree that it actually was like a rushing
mighty wind, and, more than filling just a house, it filled the
entire open space of the Circo and extended beyond, coursing
through the numerous backstreets, carrying to the outskirts
of the Eternal City, drifting into windows and corridors and
caverns, prompting Triboulet to at last appear, entering in his
enormous ship-car, which was covered in ivy and vines, all of
which seemed to be alive, as if they were pulsing upon the mast.

When descending from the vehicle to the ground, Triboulet was accompanied by his cackle of hyenas, and a hyena
also appeared unto each member of his troupe and walked

with them as they cavorted, continuing to blow upon their flutes, drawing people into the heart of Circo Massimo. When the performers and the crowd started to blend, the infectious, near hysterical high-pitched laughter of the hyenas filled everyone present as Triboulet's fierce laugh carried through the air, the spirit of the hyenas provoking in them an almost convulsive response, the animal's laughter rippling through their bodies, streaming into them like some primordial force, overtaking them like an epidemic. Now when this was noised about Rome, the multitude came together, and no longer did they speak, but laugh and laugh and laugh, each laugh quite unlike every other, as if each were a different language, though laughter transcended logos, for one didn't laugh through language but the body, and the musicians imitated the sound of the hyena's laughter on their instruments, though it was mostly those with wind instruments that did so while those with drums and cymbals heightened the entire *pandemonious* din with thunderous calls and responses, the boom and crash of their instruments reaching ecstatic crescendos, at which point Triboulet clambered up the mast of his ship-car and blowing upon his *salpinx*, produced a sharp, cutting, lucid sound that focused everyone, drawing attention to him as the tremulous note of his extended trumpet hovered in the air.

Gazing at the crowd through his mask, the enigmatic jongleur announced:

Let me please introduce myself, I'm a man of jests and japes, then knelt on the ground and digging his hands into the soil proclaimed: *Ecce Humus!* as the soil cascaded through his hands: Behold the Earth and the gifts that it provides for us.

We are *autochthons*: those who spring from the earth and the earth alone, making his first truly public address, for his other pronouncements were made in near privacy, only amongst his troupe, though the kids were present when he first arrived, but how and in what way they received his words or actions wasn't known.

Let us celebrate this day with a feast, with but some of the many fruits of the earth, for this is a time of celebration. The harvest time is upon us! *Ecce Humus!*

Walking to the head of Circo Massimo and approaching the altar, behind which three aged women from the troupe sat in scarlet gowns, Triboulet knelt before them as the clouds above parted and rays of light encircled them, their faces, despite their advanced age, radiant and sensual, suffused with an entrancing beauty, their gaze hypnotic and arresting.

How not better to celebrate the harvest time than by honoring women? Once, I believed in many strange, disturbing things, but I learned much from them about life and the body, for they possess knowledge that men do not—how they taught me to love the body and all its fecundity, its processes of life and death, of which there is nothing unclean, just as there is nothing unclean in this soil. To 'soil' is not to defile or pollute—let us cleanse ourselves of such perversions with the *solum* itself!

And stripping naked, though not removing his mask, Triboulet took handfuls of the soil from the ground and rubbed it on his chest, and then as he stretched out his arms perpendicular to the earth as if to begin one of his spinning dances, the earth cascading from his hands, the three aged women approached him and began covering his body with the soil, washing it, rubbing the matter over his shoulders, back, and buttocks, and as they took handfuls of the moist earth and rubbed it over his genitals, the aged women gazed outwards and chanted in unison in soprano:

O foolish philosophers, O theological asses, O preachers of asininities! What have ye against matter?! *Amor solum! Amor solum! Amor solum!*

After they finished cleansing Triboulet, the aged women returned to their places behind the altar; three hyenas followed suite. Walking over the backs of their benches, the animals sat directly behind them—they appeared to grow right out of their very bodies, as if they were extensions of their shoulders and the crowns of their heads, poised as they were just above them.

The midgets then rolled out the beehive barrels and distributed to all present flagons with *hydromeli* as Triboulet seized a crushed red velvet drape from the altar and, drawing it away, revealed an abundance of pine cones, blackberries, and watermelons.

After wrapping the velvet drape around his body, Triboulet took a watermelon, smashed it open, then said:

Take of this succulent fruit, it is of the earth and, like us, it is composed mostly of water, and, like us, it is sweet and satisfying, as refreshing as a lover on a hot Sunday afternoon.

And all came forward to partake of the watermelons, cracking them open and sharing pieces of the fleshy fruit with those around them while the kids streamed throughout Circo Massimo, chasing the monkeys, trying to catch them to put them in the swings, which they finally did, albeit only through the monkeys acquiescing; although they enjoyed being pushed back and forth in the swings, they didn't remain in them for long since, what are swings to masters of swinging like monkeys? Leaping from the swings out of the kids' reach, the monkeys ran around the arena, snatching watermelon rinds out of people's hands, throwing flowers about, tossing pine cones here and there, and instigating havoc, after which they leapt onto the sculpture that the troupe had been working on for weeks and which they had covered whenever they finished working. As the monkeys climbed over and about the mysterious object, circling it in every direction, scampering up its side swiftly and with unerring agility, they started tearing holes in the fabric, and with each tear, the holes grew wider and wider; then the monkeys began swinging from the torn pieces of fabric, tearing more and more of it away until, at last, the sculpture was completely devoid of its shroud. Rushing before it, everyone recognized that, although it wasn't completely defined, it resembled the shape of a man, or so they believed, making them presume that the troupe was sculpting a statue of Triboulet — all twisted around to face him and exulted, "Triboulet! Triboulet! Triboulet!" which made him turn abruptly and stare at them with terrible ferocity and pronounce in a chilling tone, his words searing like hot arrows: —

Do not make an idol of me! What if your reverence should some day collapse? Be careful lest a statue fall and kill you! The time of idols has come and gone. Come, let us destroy that which we divinize, for all that we divinize destroys us in the end!

Leading them to the altar, Triboulet approached it vigilantly and, with a gesture, signaled to the aged women seated behind it, prompting them to rise and, pushing the altar apart, expose the benches that each of them were sitting on, revealing that they were made of the trees that the people had been venerating, for they contained the burn marks from the lightning, and the people were astonished — the trunks of each tree were carved into seats and the remainder of the venerated objects were piled behind them in a large triangular heap.

Calling the people forward, Triboulet invited each of them to take a torch and set aflame the trunks and branches, but they were full of trepidation, even trembled at what he bid them do, with many protesting, angrily declaiming the troupe's having desecrated the objects.

As they hesitated and recoiled before his task, gazing at him in fear and continuing to protest, the women rushed forward and affixed a tail, enormous phallus, and donkey mask to Triboulet, then kicked and kicked him in the ass, laughing at the fool as he hee-hawed and hee-hawed, braying, kicking, leaping, baring his teeth and tongue until one of the kids leapt upon his back and he trotted about, the goats, monkeys, and hyenas all mingling around as he began to speak in a high pitched voice: Who do you say that I am? And the people shouted, "The great Triboulet! Master of the streets! New King of Rome!" to which he countered: What's to revere? Call me this, call me that, but, am I to be venerated? Some call me Triboulet, some Asterios, yet others call me Chthonios — am I he, Omadios, Punch, or simply ... *Hanswurst*? I'm just a happy go lucky clown, I hardly ever wear a frown, you could

adjust your point of view. Am I—Cush? Kish? Tseih She?
Ra's al-ghūl? a donkey?! O bla de-i-ty, ib liss da-da-i-ty?
Pleased to meet you, hope you guess my name …

And as he hee-hawed and hee-hawed, the hyenas laughed
and nudged him, the women kept kicking him in the ass, the
monkeys threw watermelon rinds at him, and the kids continuously pelted him with blackberries and dung, but when
the three aged women tried to king the enigmatic jongleur, a
monkey quickly snatched the crown from his head and threw
it onto the heap of branches and trunks and leapt up and down,
pointing at the heap and screeching; in the midst of the havoc
one of the kids grabbed a torch and threw it against the heap:
— quickly, the flames took hold, for the wood was covered with
a light coating of tar and the fire was seductive, prompting
others to approach the heap and touch it with their torches,
till at last everyone came forward and added to the fire, the
flames leaping into the sky with delight, the wood cracking
and snapping in the night, which had just begun to emerge.

When the kids witnessed a group of young men in white
vestments gazing from the side of Circo Massimo in astonishment at the fire, they ran towards them and in a frenzy,
dragged them inside the Circo and while laughing and giggling, as if in possession of some prodigious strength, stripped
them of all their clothes, which they promptly threw upon
the fire, then rolled the young men in the soil, taking handfuls of it, rubbing it all over them, shoving it in their mouths,
washing them with it and, though they didn't know what they
were saying, chanted AMOR SOLUM! just like the women,
after which they tore off their own clothes to wash themselves

with the soil, too, which reminded them of birds fluttering in dirt, and their unharnessed abandon spurred others to do the same, and the troupe accompanied their revels with simple but hypnotic & thunderous drumbeats, intensifying the rhythms as the entire crowd began to undress and cleanse themselves with the soil while the three aged women carried before the fire a large basket overflowing with lilies. After emptying the flowers on the ground, they began slowly mincing them with their hands, joyfully tearing the pure white flowers to pieces, and others joined in the act as the women produced more & more baskets of the flowers until everyone was tearing them to pieces; once they finished, the remnants were cast onto the fire, instantaneously burning as the tongues of the flames snapped, cracked, incinerating the bits of stems and petals until the smell of burnt lilies pervaded the air and everyone began chanting: *Amor solum! Amor solum! Amor solum!*

Picking up thin bundles of pine branches that were strewn throughout the Circo, all frolicked alongside Tribou-let's ship-car, waving the branches as he and the troupe fes-ted everyone out of the arena and to Villa Pamphili, with all continuing to repeatedly chant AMOR SOLUM! as they traversed the streets, anointed with soil, until they arrived at the labyrinth, around which were strewn belladonna, hen-bane, and sunflowers as well as numerous vast horn-shaped wicker baskets overflowing with pomegranates, which the troupe distributed to everyone, as well as to the goats in par-ticular, for they delighted in the bittersweet arils and nibbled fiendishly at the rough skin of the fruit until reaching the cherished seeds.

Enjoying as they did the company of the goats, the kids teased them, tossing pomegranates back and forth, making the animals chase them, and when one pomegranate was cast into the far distance and the goats ran after it, the kids followed them, as did one of the trombonists, for he heard what he thought was a familiar sound, and when the goats began to bleat wildly, the trombonist pushed past them to see what provoked the animals only to discover a flautist fornicating with a percussionist. Furious, he invited the other members of the troupe to see what to him was an "obscene sight, such shame enchained!" Calling Triboulet forward, the trombonist shouted, "This is adultery! Are we to stand for this? Let's cast her from the troupe!"

Bemused by the musician's attitude, Triboulet said astonished: *Adultery?*

"She's my wife!"

If I was present at your wedding, I would have exercised *ius primae noctis* with her, but did we not abandon all such vows? Once, and for some recidivists it remains the same, it was adulterous even to marry anew after divorcing one's wife, and some believe that the Hebrew even advocated castration —would you follow that precept, too, like Origen, and make self-castration preferable to 'impurity'?

Give us his balls!

He's only got one!

It's not a ball; it's an ingrown swollen pudendum!

He's a hermaphrodite—the best of both worlds!

Many a philosopher would like to screw him, *er, her, er, ahhh* ... the god!

Or would you rather keep your balls, and say bollocks to eunuchs and old rotten fathers who know not the wisdom of the body, juſt as she should keep her balls and taſte whatever delights her, for, have not you also enjoyed the fruits of *many* others?

The trombonist remained silent before Triboulet, then, as if devoid of control, as if possessed by some force deeply ingrained in his body deſpite having believed he expunged it, he began fuming, cursing "obscene!" and "shame!" as if he were going to ſtone her.

Turning to the reſt of the troupe Triboulet said: Come, let us be more magnanimous — is not monogamy for … *monotheiſts?!*

Forget innocence, forget adultery, what is truly unforgivable is unacted desires—give us experience! Only ripe fruit is edible!

"*Obscenity! Shame!*"

I would hope and pray that such 'obscenity' and 'shame' might be my lot! Who would not want to frolic with a woman as fair as this flautiſt! She can *flaut* me whenever she wishes, and in any orifice she wants!

Triboulet's rejoinder, completely devoid of solemnity, provoked the laughter of the reſt of the troupe, who seized the tromboniſt upon his urging, and the flautiſt and the percussioniſt returned to their pleasures, provoking the goats to begin indulging in their own, and everyone observed them screwing, meditating upon the invincible power of their sex drive, which was moſt admirable when it led to nothing and was but an expression of the aimless joy of life, the seed swallowed or given to the entrails, but when the kids began imitating the goats, everyone burst into hysterical laughter, save for the trombonist, who remained as solemn as ever.

Come, let's take him to the maze!

When they reached the labyrinth, in silence, the three aged women began circling it, censing the structure with large bundles of sage and shooting fluid from their breasts onto the ground.

Once the women completed their ritual, Triboulet stood before the entrance to the labyrinth and picking up a sledge hammer, struck the stone with a formidable blow, shattering it perfectly in half. After the two large porphyry blocks were moved to the side, opening the passageway, Triboulet shattered the tablet-like objects into further pieces and the newly arriving goats stepped onto the stones, perching themselves on the sharp broken shards as if they were standing atop mountain peaks. Edging forward, all gathered before the gateway, and Triboulet called out to the troupe, whom brought forth the trombonist, and with *terribilità*, the masked one chanted in a tongue unknown to most, if not all, and directed the trombonist into the labyrinth, his voice escalating in pitch and intensity as the musician hesitantly and with considerable fear approached the doorway. Joining Triboulet, the other members of the troupe began chanting as well, making a myriad of frightening, primitive percussive noises with their mouths, clicking their tongues against their teeth and palates, till the trombonist tentatively crossed the threshold of the labyrinth, moving into the darkness pervading it, not knowing which way to turn, which path to take, not knowing, too, what was within it …

Seizing a goat as the troupe continued to chant, Triboulet quickly snapped its neck, chopped its head off, then tore
out its entrails and swiftly caſt the ſteaming organs upon the
ground. Other goats were seized and sacrificed and prepared
for cooking as he gazed into the organs, their folds, twiſts,
turns, and convolutions an echo of the disjointed, confusing
pathways of the labyrinth, its lengthy hallways interminable,
myſterious wandering places.

Reflected in them, Triboulet witnessed not only the journey of the trombonist through the maze, but also other events,
and in the darkness he saw visions of the desecration of the Old
City of Jerusalem as well as the thievery of the bells and the
wrapping of Canterbury Cathedral; as the chanting persiſted,
intensified, grew more feral and ferocious, volatile, monſtrous,
even horrific, other visions came to him, too, manifeſting in
the entrails, juſt as the images of hiſtory were unveiled to him
like phantasmagoric pictures from a kaleidoscope, and he saw
a hill in northern Lithuania densely encruſted with crosses,
giant crucifixes, ſtatues of the Virgin Mary and thousands of
tiny effigies all burſt into flames, which engulfed the pilgrim-
age site as if it were saturated with gasoline, shooting upwards
and out, even, it seemed, *into* the earth, and he could smell the
acrid and aſphyxiating scent of burnt metal, wood, plaſtic, and
other materials as he watched the oſtentatious and baroque
mise-en-scène disintegrating in the fire, and it coalesced with
horrid screams and the sound of a tributary violently overflowing, moonlight shimmering on the water, as it did on the walls
of the labyrinth, out of which aggressively issued the hyenas,
from whose mouths bits of what resembled raw meat were

dangling, but in the darkness it was difficult to discern exactly
what was clutched between their teeth, just as one is never
sure whether visions are actual events, imagined scenarios one
desires to see enacted, or mere explosions of irrational images,
like dreams quickly forgotten, never remembered, recalled, or
at all corresponding to any reality, as far as one understands,
but it was clear that the hyenas were clutching some kind of
meat between their teeth just as the statue of the archbishop
was hanging from his feet and the

?

had replaced the image of Christ Pantocrator and the smell
of seasoned goat wafted through the air, its seared, tasty flesh
attracting one and all, and everyone gathered together and
partook of the meat, roasted tomatoes, and onions, while
even the bees that prompted Triboulet's arrival were feasting
upon a still barely breathing dove, its body trembling, wings
fluttering, foam seeping out its mouth, light tremors shattering its fragile head against the ground as the bees piped away,
z-e-e-p, z-e-e-p, zeep, zeep, and the kids drew hyenas in the
soil with sticks to the accompaniment of the midgets' laughter.

Standing before one and all, Triboulet proclaimed:

Is the nature of my game puzzling you? Let us love this
world, and the things that are in this world. Today is a new
day, the day of a new dawn, the day of the *solum* and the laugh.

It has been a *witty* day — let us remember it from this moment forward, though, in the future, days will be measured anew. To the hyena!

Early the next morning, while en route to SS Giovanni, just before the sun began to rise, a priest discovered that the Arch of Constantine had been tightly wound with black polyamide. When the sun streaked through the fabric, it created a shadow on the ground which read:

Ceci n'est pas un Christ

KINGDOM
TIDE

Catholic authorities the world over were filled with increasing alarm as the desecration of their religious sites continued with greater and greater intensity, for Triboulet's vision of the burning hill of crosses did in fact correspond to reality, just as did his vision of a violently overflowing tributary—while Šiauliai, Joniškis, and the surrounding cities were suffering from a blackout for nearly one month, unbeknownst to local authorities, who were embroiled in policing the havocking citizens and tending to other emergency situations, a dam had been constructed on the nearby Kulvė River, a tributary to the Mūša River, which led to the hill of crosses and the surrounding area being suddenly and entirely submerged in over ten feet of water, prompting many citizens to presume that the end was nigh, though others believed that, despite the crosses & *alia* having already been totally incinerated, when the flood followed the fire, it was "the hand of God" intervening in the disaster. State officials concurred that, just as in Kent, England, the blackout was not organic but engineered and presumably committed by the same and still unidentified culprits behind the thievery of the bells, for all of the churches in the area had been divested of their bells, too. In addition, the near exact similarity between the message on the billboard in Damascus and the fabric engulfing the Arch of Constantine led the Papacy to postulate that, although it may have been comprised of many members, there was a single anti-clerical organization or faction behind the act and, most likely, the same people were undoubtedly responsible for the numerous incidents of vandalism committed against the different sacred Catholic sites around the world. Subsequent to discovering the funereally shrouded Arch, the priest also found numerous large stone letters scattered around the base of the monument; at first, he thought that they were only displaced remnants from one of the surrounding ancient sites, the result of uncouth tourists shamelessly amusing themselves, but upon closer examination the blocks of letters and diacritical marks seemed to be fragments from law tablets of some kind. Quite far from the innocuous pranks of mere art school students or eco-terrorists, *in toto*, the acts were considered by the Papacy to be not merely grievous instances of sacrilege committed by immoderate heathens, or merely polemical atheists of a radical bent, but an unequivocal declaration of war, perhaps by Islamic extremists, for the pope believed that "Mohammed brought nothing that was new, only evil and inhuman things, such as his command to spread by the sword the faith he preached," citing Byzantine emperor Manuel Palaiologos to embolden his view. The enigmatic character of each of the crimes was too what led papal authorities to regard them as indicative of something more ominous than mere acts of vandalism, for the Aramaic message contained in the black polyamide fabric had been decoded, but, while announcing it was a matter of "special concern," and a convocation was being held to address it, the content of the message was not revealed to the public, which betrayed the terrible gravity with which the Vatican viewed it, or at very least their exceeding caution, or some stratagem, and the fabric and the scholars who had deciphered it were being kept under strict and constant supervision. Although far from as extreme or pervasive, the incidents were for many reminiscent of the dechristianization campaign enacted during the French

Revolution, provoking the Papacy to issue stern warnings that it would not suffer religious intolerance of any kind, or the confiscation of any of its remaining properties, let alone the murder of its worldly representatives, and that whoever was involved in the crimes would be prosecuted to the fullest extent of the law by an international tribunal according to the *jus gentium*, though the "ultimate judgment" of the culprits would rest with "the Supreme Being and the Supreme Being alone." In strict concord with the Papacy, the ruling bodies of the U.N. affirmed that they would fully cooperate in the pursuit and prosecution of the criminals, as did, too, the Great Sovereign Body of the Joint Chiefs of Staff of the U.S. Government, who issued a statement regarding the crimes, which closed with the promise that, "while God blesses America alone, America, we assure you, guarantees the safety of every territory in the world, for just as God is our Father, we are yours." Finding this a moment for an ever intensified renewal of faith, the pope urged believers to recall that those who fight in the name of God are recognized as *Milites Christi*, warriors or knights of Christ, and that victory would be achieved through divine intervention or aid from God. Although it may have suffered a significant wound and lost much of its political power during the French Revolution and other later skirmishes and polemics, paradoxically, the church had ultimately proven to be impregnable, regardless of the veracity of the various accusations leveled against it and regardless of the scientific facts displacing its fantastical views of the cosmos, the formation and age of the earth, the evolution of human beings, etc., for it is a 2000 years old unscratchable *petra*, a stone-sponge absorbing everything, even dinosaur bones and pedophiliac scandals, and even if it continued to lose certain battles, in the end, it would prove invincible and "win the war." Such proclamations found fervent and fanatical support amongst believers, suffusing with incendiary passion preachers and prophets, many of whom saw in the cataclysms of their epoch the signs of the coming of the end, just as had the preachers and prophets of every previous age, yet despite the fact that since the death of Christ the end of time had still yet to come, they shouted and declaimed from the streets and the rooftops, with one preacher in Piazza del Popolo railing furiously that

"the time is fulfilled, and the Kingdom of God is at hand: REPENT, YE, AND BE-LIEVE THE GOSPEL! Do you not see? The signs of the coming of the end are upon us! The sun has darkened, the moon has not given her light, the stars have fallen from the sky, and the celestial powers are shaking! Do you not hear the lamenta-tions of the peoples of the world?

Nations are warring against na-tions, lightning has struck from east to west, and there be famines and earthquakes and plagues— all these things are the first birth pangs of the new age! Remember the words of the prophet Daniel: 'When you see the abomination of desolation, know that the end is nigh!' But we will not run to the hills; we will fight!"

And it was Triboulet and his troupe in particular that were seen by some as that abomination, despite their not being implicated in any crime, nor even being found in areas remote to the crimes, and the preacher urged the people not to follow them, for "they are of the devil's brethren, and even if they seem to provide comfort and relief, laughter is not the way of the Lord, nor the kind of relief believers should seek. ,Alas,'" the preacher roared, intoxicated by spiritual fire-water, "remember the words of Luke: ,Woe unto you that laugh now! for ye shall mourn and weep.' They who sow in laughter, shall reap in tears. Cursed be the man that trusteth in man! Know ye not that the unrighteous shall not inherit the kingdom of God? Be not deceived: neither fornicators, nor idolaters, nor adulterers, nor effeminate, nor abusers of themselves with mankind. Nor thieves, nor covetous, nor drunkards, nor revilers, nor extortioners shall inherit the kingdom of God. Unless ye REPENT ye shall likewise perish! Remember the words of the Christ: ,I came not to call the righteous, but sinners to repentance!' Remember the fate of sinners! They shall lick the dust like a serpent, they shall move out of their holes like worms of the earth: they shall be afraid of the LORD our God, and shall fear because of thee."

While the prophets and preachers continued to fulminate, attempting to foment disgust, rage, fear, and enact vengeance, proselytizing about the end times and the destruction of the world, beleaguered by the pestiferous moral fervor, Triboulet left Piazza del Popolo and decided to refresh himself in one of the fountains at Piazza Farnese after viewing Carracci's fresco cycle and his *Triumph of Bacchus and Ariadne*. Submerging himself in the brisk water, he remained beneath the surface, savoring the silence and solitude, meditating on the irrationality of the fear of divine wrath as he watched the dance of bright, sparkling star-like points of sunlight on the surface of the water, which seemed to morph suddenly and swiftly as if hundreds of years were fleeting by.

Emerging from the fountain, he startled three women

walking through the piazza, especially because of his mask, which made them think he was some kind of demon, but he was even more startled himself when encountering the gaze of the mesmerizing woman in the center, who was dressed in white and had emerald eyes. Her salutation, which he returned, suffused him with such lasting ecstasy despite the brevity of the encounter, and after returning to Villa Pamphili to enjoy a siesta beside his labyrinth, he fell asleep thinking of that enchanting woman, only his eyes remained open, and in that wide-awake state of sleep, a vision was presented to him: "In a cave which I once often frequented, a mist the color of fire appeared to me, within which I discerned a bearded figure with a fearsome aspect to such as should gaze upon him, but who seemed to rejoice inwardly that it was a marvel to see. Unbeknownst to him, he was accompanied by two tigers and a retinue of jovial, laughing figures who made wide circles around him, watching him from the shadows, intervening in his acts, exerting influence from afar. Directing me through a mountain forest, he led me to a secluded grove where a person was sleeping, covered only with a crimson cloth; upon whom looking very attentively, I knew that it was the enchanting woman, who had been compelled to salute me, despite her fear. And he who led me to her held also in his hand a thing that was burning in flames, and he said to me 'Behold thy heart.' But when he had remained with me a little while, I saw him awaken the woman, after which he urged her to eat the organ which flamed in his hand; and she ate as one fearing."

It was not clear for how long Triboulet slept, but after he awoke, he began climbing a mountain and at its summit, after passing through an intense fire, he came upon a series of "eyes," for that is what he called mountain lakes, and while at the summit, he witnessed twenty-four bearded men drowning and four animals with six wings as plumage attempting to save them, but they too were drowned in the eyes of the summit. As he watched them perish, he heard the sounds of a terrified woman, which made him turnabout, whereupon he witnessed a chariot on two wheels bearing the woman, but the strange animal that was drawing the chariot on vanished as the earth cracked open beneath it. Seizing the woman, who now gazed upon Triboulet with dread, he scaled the side of the mountain, crisscrossing it like a crab, and as he descended, moving closer and closer to the ground, she witnessed others perishing, including a lone old man prone to hallucinatory projections, and before reaching the base of the mountain, the chariot came tumbling over and with a great thundering crack, burst into hundreds of pieces, shattering as if made of petrified wood. Carrying her back to the labyrinth, when he laid her on the ground, he was astonished by her attire, which was that of another century, but also by a sense of purity that emanated from her, that there was something *unripe* in her, and he called upon the three aged women and whispered to them a series of instructions.

Deep in an unknown wood, the woman with the emerald eyes awoke to the sound of frightening drums, double flutes, chanting, bells, and cymbals. Full of terror, she watched as Triboulet's retinue danced, leaping about a fire with visceral abandon, the masked men and women dressed in satyr and maenad costumes, gleefully flipping their heads back and forth, delighting in the different shapes of their bodies and the animal din of night. She thought that she was in the inferno, that she had perhaps died, but it was not true—this was not the end of the world, it was the very beginning. Bound as she was to a tree, Beatrice could not escape, and as the music intensified and the troupe imbibed some nectar, caterpillars fell from the branches above her, dropping to the ground, twisting and curling, attempting to inch their way to safety, some even falling on her, crawling along her limbs, their soft, furry, minuscule legs making her flesh tingle and shiver as, closing in on her, the masked figures danced in ever tighter and tighter circles until several members of the troupe broke from the circle and unbound her, but even though quite strong, when she tried to flee, she could not escape, as she was trapped within a tight circle bound by yet another circle, bound by yet another circle, bound by yet another circle, each twisting and turning in different directions, each varying their speeds, their bodies firmly locked together, creating unbreakable chains, until three figures broke from the innermost ring and two of them seized Beatrice's arms as another poured the nectar into her mouth, but, fight as she did, she could not resist swallowing the liquid, for it continued to flow and flow, surging out of the flagon with such force that she had to swallow as much of it as she could, otherwise she'd choke, and she refused to let herself die, because she thought it would be too akin to suicide, "a mortal sin," and whatever she could not drink spilled over her, washing over her face and body, saturating her clothing, at which point the dancers began to widen the circles and when the three figures broke away, the one smashing the flagon against a tree, all of the circles broke apart and turned upon her, tearing her clothes from her till she was completely naked, whereupon the members of the troupe began chanting: *Amor solum! Amor solum! Amor solum!* as she covered herself in shame, and seizing handfuls of soil, the women started to cleanse Beatrice, rubbing it over her arms, breasts, stomach, back, and buttocks, and as she trembled and wept before them, not knowing of her fate, she called upon the Lord, but there was no answer, and after everyone disrobed and cleansed themselves in the moist soil, they continued drinking more and more till they were in a euphoric state, and to the wet crash of cymbals, while entranced, the women of the troupe began to douse Beatrice's body with liquid from the flagons until it penetrated her pores, then danced around the fire with her, tossing her back and forth between them, once delirious, stopping, they then covered the ground with animal skins and laid her upon them and rubbed her body with oils until she began to acquiesce, surrendering to the sustained sensual caresses of the women, who suddenly but slowly started penetrating her with *olisboi* and *godemiches*, her shocked body trembling as they entered each of her orifices, the spasms rippling through her flesh as blood erupted from between her legs and flowed over her loins, after which they carried her to an even deeper recess in the woods where between two trees Triboulet awaited her.

After standing on his head and jutting his legs into the air, the women carried Beatrice over to him, then lifted her on top of the masked figure as his legs rested against their bodies and he caressed them, searching inside the folds of their flesh while Beatrice released herself, slowly, rhythmically, her senses pulsing, her breath deepening, extending, sweat gushing out of her, her flesh finally awakening, coalescing with Triboulet's as other members of the troupe tore a goat to pieces, its violent shrieks blending with the cacophony of the music, and locking his legs around her, he lowered himself to the ground while she held him within her, and kneeling behind her, he engulfed her, drawing her closer to him, suffusing her, and as she felt the black goat skin rubbing against her flesh, in an even greater frenzy, she reached back to grab his head so as to pull him tighter against her, felt horns emerging from him—seized them bodies convulsed groaning trembling in terror grunting limbs shaking shrieks blood rushing into mouths complete release: — surrendering to the animal tearing her to pieces, rollicking against her flesh pulsing united beast-human — erupting white flares, sight lost, bones loosed inside bodies melding into the very earth beneath dying consciously, the noises of the ritual, reenacted over a period of numerous days, fading into oblivion ~

When she awoke, the three aged women dressed her anew, blindfolded her, compacted her ears and nose with wax, then escorted her from their haunt to Villa Pamphili, where the blindfold and wax were both removed to the accompaniment of the troupe's music. As she stood before Triboulet, although different, he sensed that she was not completely transformed, and when he circled her like an animal and smelt her, he knew that deep within her cells there remained something … *regressive*. Turning to the troupe, he lifted three saxophones to his mouth and produced a note that he rarely ever sounded. At that moment, the troupe began playing *Kýrie, eléison*, and after performing several bars, a tear welled up from the corner of her right eye and her shoulders trembled slightly. Sounding another note, Triboulet prompted the troupe to repeat a symmetrical tritone divided by minor thirds, first on a single flute, then a bassoon, flugelhorn, and saxophone, and as they continued playing, each troupe member joining in on different instruments, Triboulet approached her and whispered in her ear, his beard scratching her neck: *If you know the way through the celestial realms, do you know your way through the labyrinth?* then thrust her with ferocity towards the entrance, everyone chanting, making frightening, primitive percussive noises with their mouths, clicking their tongues against their teeth and palates, smashing cymbals together, clanging brake drums, thumping tam-tams, gongs, and anvils, drumming temple blocks, striking claves, shaking maracas, cracking whips, rubbing güiros and shouting and shrieking at certain intervals, punctuating off-beats as she entered the labyrinth, moving into the darkness that pervaded it, not knowing which way to turn, which path to take, not knowing, too, what was within it, the folds, twists, turns and convolutions of the labyrinth concealing its mysteries. She sensed something foreboding in the walls as well—in walking between them, their force pressed upon her with considerable weight, disorienting her, disturbing her balance, disrupting her physiological orientation as she paced through their corridors, continuing in what seemed to be nearly straight lines, but as she walked along them, the lines evaporated around subtle curves, and turning along one wall she moved in the

dark, following a sliver of moonlight that shot down the pathway, but to a *cul-de-sac*. Turning back, she retraced her steps,
and walking along another path, this one not at all illuminated,
she crept along, step by step, then followed a curving wall
round and round, the darkness inky and dense, and stepping
forward, as some indiscernible but eerie sound echoed through
the chambers, she came to a dead end. Turning back yet once
more, as she attempted to follow a new path, she wanted to
peer above the walls, but they were too high, and as she continued onward with trepidation, the sense of distance between
herself and any portion of the surrounding wall altered, intensifying her disorientation, for while spatially she was aware of
where she was, simultaneously, she was lost, lucidity and
strangeness fusing, but she continued along, tracing a curving
wall round and round and round, the ferocious music of the
troupe seeping through the walls, which made her unsure as
to whether the eerie sound she'd heard before issued from
within the labyrinth itself, or from the troupe, and she continued walking as the music echoed past her, reverberating between the porphyry, and the passageway never seemed to end
until she came to an opening where four different paths lay
before her: — following one, she traced it around only to come
to another *cul-de-sac*; turning about, she followed the wall,
came to one more *cul-de-sac*; turning back, she chose a new
path, which curved slightly, the walls closing in upon her, as if
narrowing to a close, only to open again: to a blunt wall that
evoked velocity, but instead of turning around it, she went 'forward' and around another wall, which curved outward and to
the left, then bent around, and she proceeded along, shifting

uncannily between states of familiarity and alienation, but felt as if this time she was pursuing an interminable corridor that would lead to … *what?* She did not know, but to a place she felt she now had to encounter, and the lengthy corridor stretched on until she came to a juncture at which she turned, though it was one that she felt she traveled along before, but it wasn't possible to know, so she went onward and the walls began to narrow, even, it seemed, to grow, to stretch higher into the dark sky as if melding with it, and the terrestrial and the celestial realms became one, thus, there was no celestial realm for her any longer, and coming upon what seemed to be the end of the corridor she heard a terrifying noise—hesitating there, at what was a decisive curve, she thought that moment of Triboulet rising out of the fountain and of the sensation of abandonment, of the euphoria that flooded through her corpuscles when the women penetrated all of her orifices and her veins were electrified, and she could sense the heat of the fire as the thunderous clamor of the troupe's music and the primitive percussive din escalated and rushed through the corridors of the labyrinth:—at that moment, she did not care if she perished, felt in fact that she must perish, that something within her had to die, and, turning the bend, she went on, the walls, narrowing even more, almost closing, and she stood before what was like a tight doorway, faced a curved wall, around which bent two paths, the darkness on each path briefly illuminated by the glare of the moon as the clouds above broke apart, then closed, shutting out the light, and that eerie noise she'd heard earlier suddenly sounded again:—she moved towards it, walking between the ever tightening walls until she turned directly into one of the two chambers of the labyrinth and, immobilized, fearful, full of unsettling awe, stood transfixed before a minotaur … As the human-beast turned towards her, she remembered hearing of the wrathful *l'infamïa di Creti*, and as it snorted and groaned, its hoofs clacking against the labyrinth floor, turning its head askance, it gazed at her in almost as much wonder, for her emerald eyes were mesmerizing, and as it continued to look upon her and step closer towards her, trembling, she opened her arms to invite the creature into her flesh, to surrender to it, at which point she heard the melody of the *Kýrie, eléison*, but no tear fell from her eye, nor did she tremble, and with a swiftness undetected by her, the creature suddenly revealed itself— gazing upon him, she shuddered, her entire body quivering as he whispered into her ear, his rough chin scratching her flesh, his lips grazing it, slowly opening and closing as he gently uttered each word: *I am excruciatingly near yet I am completely absent* … and taking her body into his, she felt the sky plummeting, felt as if the earth had been unchained from the sun and was plunging continually, backward, sideward, forward, in all directions, till she wondered whether there was still any up or down and if she was not perhaps straying as if through an infinite nothing, the breath of empty space coursing through her as it became colder and colder and night continually closed in upon her and she heard the noise of gravediggers, their shovels breaking through rock with ease, and she smelt something decomposing, an odor unlike any she had ever encountered before, the stench of some sublime monster, but she knew that this death, the result perhaps of a murder, or sacrifice, was necessary, and that there would be water in which to cleanse herself of the murder, there would be festivals of atonement, sacred games that would be invented in order to overcome the sacrifice, for it was a great deed, a deed perhaps even too great, but subsequent to it would be a new, more glorious era, a higher history, and, though trembling, she was also cheerful, for the spectacle to which she was witness was evidence of some new sun seeming to have set, of some ancient and profound trust having at last turned into doubt for her, and that dying thing was like an enormous, complex but grotesque edifice, one constructed over centuries, and she watched as it collapsed, and just like the chariot that came tumbling over the mountain side burst into hundreds of pieces with a thundering crack, this baroque edifice also shattered as if made of petrified wood————— stretched in the contradiction between today and tomorrow, she felt like one belonging to a new century and free of worry and fear, a scarcely describable kind of light, happiness, relief, exhilaration, and encouragement cascaded over her, for a new dawn seemed to shine upon her, and her heart overflowed with gratitude, amazement, premonitions, expectation. At long last, the horizon appeared free, despite the fact that it was not wholly bright, and a voyage clearly awaited her, but she would venture out to face any danger, full of the daring of the lover of knowledge, and she heard the sound of the sea erupting, waves crashing upon rocks, salty water splashing up and into the air and vanishing back into itself, ever receding and advancing, the pull of the tides drawing it this way and that, and as she gazed upon the shore, she knew that the earth had no direction except that which she wished to give it, and recognizing that she came out of the sea and the earth, she remembered the chant uttered during her initiation and repeated it into the night: *Amor solum! Amor solum! Amor solum!*

The disjointed, confused pathways of the labyrinth were no longer mysterious wandering places to her, for she knowingly walked through the lengthy, interminable passages. As she approached the exit, she watched as several lizards scurried across the walls, moving as if gravity had no hold on them, and their magnificent colors glistened like the plagioclase crystals of the porphyry, which reflected the moon's vivid argentum luminosity, and she saw Triboulet and the three aged women awaiting her as they gazed toward the entrance and exit to the labyrinth, for there was only one way into it and one way out of it, if one returned from the journey. When she crossed the threshold, the troupe erupted *dal niente*, and to the clang of cymbals and rush of flutes, Triboulet crowned her with an ivy-wreath and inaugurated her into their fold, bestowing upon her the name *Aurora* and everyone chanted:

To the mistress of the labyrinth honey!

To the mistress of the labyrinth figs!

as the three aged women presented her with honey and figs and other gifts.

To celebrate her rebirth and transformation into Aurora, throughout Circo Massimo, the troupe hung cobalt and emerald banners with rose bunting and prepared a banquet table overflowing with foods, fruits, and other delights. When she and Triboulet arrived, the stadium was lined with large

bright burning torches and people were being rocked in the
swings as some members of the troupe engaged in acrobatics, did contortions, traipsed about on stilts, or juggled while
others performed, the musicians holding cutting contests as
one by one various people mounted Triboulet's swing, though
none of them could ever span an arc close to even half of his,
nor swing for any great duration of time, but they struggled
to do so, much to the amusement of one another and Aurora, but what especially delighted her were the kids, who
frolicked about the stadium, playing whatever games they
invented with the animals, yet what she found most comical
was when, after the kids tried to ride the hyenas like horses
and dug their feet into them like spurs, the monkeys imitated
them, yet while it was easy for the hyenas to throw the kids
from their backs, they could not do so with the primates, who
grimaced and screeched victoriously as the carnivores tried to
dislodge them, emitting low-pitched *hoo, hoo, hoos* the faster
they raced around, and the stadium was pervaded with merriment. But to inaugurate Aurora's entry into the troupe, and
as a new praxis for the coming dawn, which her transformation coincided with as if it were but one more necessary and
crucial stage leading to the anticipated transvaluation that had
been developing over millennia, Triboulet chose to institute
the agonistic practices that he had been privately engaging in
with his troupe and developing in secret. He knew that the
decisive *kairos* was at hand and the troupe would at last make
public their agonal games with an archery competition as well
as other sports. But before commencing with the founding
of the agon, the three aged women announced that Aurora

would be performing a dance, and after the troupe cleared a
space equal to the size of the labyrinth, to the sound of pipes,
tambours, and castanets, Aurora entered the stadium in a top-
less, flounced light linen dress, her hair bound in beautiful
braids, the girls beside her crowned with garlands, the men
in slightly oiled shirts, golden daggers dangling from their
silver belts, and to the clang of cymbals, the dance started
with Aurora raising her hands in the air in a circular movement as snakes undulated in them, twisting in her hands, their
tongues slithering in and out as if to kiss, and turning about,
she proceeded through a series of sinuous movements, which
all of the other dancers followed in their daedalic evolutions,
winding and unwinding like the labyrinth's pathways, or the
ecliptic, and after tossing her snakes to the ground and taking up a thyrsus, Aurora held it over the heads of the animals
that flanked her, and turning about and stamping the staff on
the ground three times, drew everyone together, each dancer
linking hands with the next until the entire procession of 50
dancers were linked and they danced in a ring, turning round
and round and round, punctuating each turn with breathy ecstatic exclamations, then, opening the ring, they all started to
dance in a line, with the dancer at each end holding a garland
in the air till, stretching their hands to the utmost limits, the
line broke— —each dancer leaping about on his or her own,
clicking, ripping, and rattling castanets, stretching their arms
apart and leaping to their toes, throwing their heads back and
forth, the men jutting their swords into the air, the women
dancing on one foot like a crane, arcing their heads back and
gazing into the sky, or shifting from foot to foot, hopping

back and forth, articulating the various sensations flowing through their bodies with precise and sharp hand gestures, sometimes placing their hands against their hips, over their heads, or to the sides of their bodies while others unloosed the fabric of their dresses and danced with it, tossing it over their shoulders or beneath their buttocks as they threw their heads back, their hair flailing in the wind as tumblers leapt, rolled, and did somersaults along the edges of Circo Massimo, and as Aurora drew everyone together once more and circled back to where the dance commenced then culminated it, Triboulet called out:

Let us honor the mistress of the labyrinth! To her who is victorious, to her who knows the winding secrets and can navigate through the darkness—Let us celebrate her triumphant apostasy! Aurora!

And bundles of myrtle twigs and casks of oil were laid at her feet as Triboulet approached the transformed one and affixed a mask to her face, the spectral colors of dawn diffusing the inky black of night, an intense range of yellows and oranges in and around the sun shimmering on the periphery of the clouds, traces of cerulean spreading across the sky, hints of emerald appearing beyond the brilliant yellow region bordering the sun, the clouds reflecting it all as wine-dark hues crested the earth's horizon.

To begin the inauguration and institute the agon in Aurora's honor, from the hull of his ship-car, Triboulet shouted: Unveil the targets! Seize your bows! ... and as it was done, he opened a hatch in the hull; out of it, a swarm of *anax imperator* dragonflies rushed, speeding through the air, soaring from one end of the stadium to the other, hovering over the banquet table like assassins waiting to strike, their long thin translucent wings feverishly fluttering in the breaking reddish sun, and they wandered north and south, east and west, stealthily pursuing their tasks. As the targets were arranged, Triboulet and Aurora watched the dragonflies in silence, both of them seeming to actually commune with the insects, if not at very least simply delight in their alacritous movements. With as much poise as the *anax imperator*, sensing the targets were at last set, Triboulet suddenly turned and standing perpendicular to one of the targets, his feet placed apart in an open stance, he pointed his bow to the ground, placed the shaft of the arrow on its rest, nocked the arrow and, opening his eyes, raised and drew his bow then, sustaining the pull for an exceedingly inordinate duration, his muscles relishing the pressure of the intensity of the draw weight, he envisioned the dawn of a new epoch, then, relaxing the fingers of his drawing hand, *fired the arrow*—cutting through the air, but perfectly still, it swiftly flew towards its target, which Triboulet imagined to be an infinite sphere, then struck the center, a point much closer to the circumference than believed.

A wicked hunter am I!—See, how far spans my bow! Only the strongest can bend it so taut— —: Now come pangs! Dangerous is *this* arrow, like no arrow, —away from here! For your own health!

Poised with equal if not greater elegance, Aurora, who unbeknownst to many practiced archery when she lived in Firenze, took up her bow, assumed an open stance, aimed, then closed her eyes, grounded her bow, placed and nocked

the arrow and raising it, deftly drew back the string then forthwith let the arrow sail—cutting through the air, but perfectly
still, swiftly, it flew to its even more precise mark, struck the
nock of Triboulet's arrow, splitting it and the fletching, crest,
and shaft into pieces but driving its point ever deeper into the
center of the target, the two points melding together, forming
one of even greater power.

Exulting in her execution, Triboulet watched as the
center of that sphere and its circumference almost seemed to
crash together, collapsing in upon one another as if sucked
out of existence, or like a Mobius strip tightening and tightening until finally evaporating as if it were actually made of
nothing but mist, or as if it had never at all ever even existed.

Continuing with their games, Triboulet, Aurora, and
the troupe staged even more complex and difficult contests,
shooting and sailing their arrows through ever tighter and
tighter circles until striving to shoot them through clay finger rings, and as their arrows volleyed forth, mellifluously
cutting the air, Triboulet and other members of the troupe
seized a group of Christians as they started brutalizing
some Protestants *en route* to church, for as the religious
vandalism continued to escalate around the world, many
Christians believed that it was not actually terrorists who
were behind the desecration of their religious sites, but
radical Protestant reformers seeking to revive Luther's
revolution, for the 515th anniversary of the nailing of his
theses to the door of the All Saints' Church in Wittenberg
was fast approaching, and they knew that the Protestants
always found their ceremonial and dramatic ritualization

of Catholicism fantastical, nothing but mere ostentatious fetishism, hence their desire to cleanse their religion of its baroque encrustations.

Holding the believers captive, Triboulet and his troupe surrounded them, locking them in ever tighter and tighter circles until they could not move at all and they trembled as if they were going to be trampled to death, or violently sacrificed, but each circle started to slowly expand, twisting and turning in different directions, until creating a sensation of vertigo, at which point the circles opened and the kids and the midgets rushed in giggling and laughing, albeit with a sinister tone, and after whirling round and round the believers and dousing them with some nectar, they leapt on them and started tearing off all their clothes until they were stripped completely naked, then rolled about in the soil and cleansed with it as everyone chanted: *Amor solum! Amor solum! Amor solum!* and the troupe sounded away on their instruments, playing a strange, powerful piece of music they'd never before performed, something so intense that the music seemed to possess *density* and like some thick ether, *entered* the very flesh, bones, and cells of whoever encountered it, altering the actual atomic structure of the body until it was transmogrified.

After turning and turning in a circle, Triboulet stood perpendicular to the believers, assumed an open stance, aimed, then closed his eyes, grounded his bow, placed and nocked the arrow and raising it, deftly drew back the string then sustaining the pull, turned towards them and spoke in a whisper as he held the arrow in its chamber, and it trembled, waiting to be released:

In my youth, I too once believed in revenge, but since that time, I circumnavigated much of the globe, and during my travels came upon many fools and madmen masquerading as saviors, but a true wise man I met at Lake Urmi spoke to me of a bridge, the bridge he said to the highest hope, a rainbow he avowed after lasting storms—*Do you want to go with us over the bridge?* To do so is to be redeemed from revenge! What you tarantulas call justice is nothing but the storm of revenge. Have you not heard? A new dawn is upon us, the age of the agon, the age of contests! As one once so full of the spirit of vengeance, I know that practices of the spirit cannot diffuse the energies of the flesh. Emotions still rage and flourish and turn in upon us, against us, resurfacing in more pernicious ways. Now, I invite you to the agon, the ground of the contest where only equals meet and where you may only have enemies that are to be hated, but not enemies to be despised. Expend your energy not in acts of vengeance against one another, but in acts of contest! Let the games begin!

As rings were drawn on the ground of the stadium and the troupe paired off the Christians and the Protestants into who they deemed the most equal opponents, the contestants were oiled up in preparation for their matches, which Triboulet and Aurora presided over as *agonothetai*. And to the crash of a cymbal, the first Christian and Protestant commenced wrestling, circling one another, wandering round the periphery of the ring, stepping towards its center, each lunging at their opponent, clinching, throwing, locking joints and breaking apart, orbiting the ring, smelling one another out like warthog and lion, till the Protestant seized the Christian and

with a sweeping curve, brought him to the ground in a direct
and immediate danger position, then pinned him and exulted,
"*Sola scriptura, sola fide!*" which made Triboulet and Aurora
burst out laughing, thus crowning the first contest with laughter and lessening the amount of wrath in the world.

And the matches continued, the Christians winning
some, the Protestants others, with the latter being generally
more adept at *par terre* and the former at standing, and while
each used a variety of moves, the Christians possessed more
brute strength and were best at gut wrenches and throws
whereas the Protestants were particularly adept at the grapevine, suplexes, and grand amplitude and throughout the contest demonstrated considerable technical superiority and grace.
Whenever the Christians would win a match, Triboulet would
shout "Tetzel!" and the kids would run up to the *agonothetai's*
table and drop three coins in a chest on the table, prompting
the troupe to form into a chorus and chant:

> *As soon as a coin in the coffer rings,*
>
> *a soul from purgatory's fire springs!*

And whenever the Protestants would win a match, Aurora would remove the coins from the coffer and throw them
back to the kids, who would then run in circles around the
Christians, round and round and round, till collapsing on
them then bursting away in a frenzy like an exploding atom
as they giggled and threw worms at the Christians, which
made Triboulet and Aurora burst into even greater spasms of
laughter.

Worms! Feed them worms! A diet of worms!

Energized by the general mirth that pervaded the ſtadium, the members of the troupe who were sculpting the enormous monument returned to their task as the competitors reſted between games. After raising the fabric that covered the bottom part of the sculpture, taking raſps and rifflers to the porphyry, the sculptors ſtarted enhancing the ſtone, shaping it into its final form, their broad, sweeping ſtrokes cutting away the excess ſtone, refining and refining it until it became clear that, beneath the foot of the figure thought to be Triboulet was a large entity of some kind which, as it was being defined, almoſt seemed to form the base of the sculpture, or at leaſt part of it, and as the sound of the sculptor's tools signaled in the ſtadium and beyond, as Triboulet, Aurora, and their troupe were inſtituting the agon and promulgating laughter, the myſterious and often enigmatic acts of deſtruction continued to proliferate throughout the world, for it was reported by the associated press that large piles of ſtromatolite were found throughout the Isle of Iona on the Inner Hebrides of Scotland, including on the grounds of Iona Abbey, and as the rocks were removed, it was discovered that each of them had been piled on top of the high crosses found on the Isle, including St. Martin's Cross, which dated to the 8th Century, and the replica of St. John's Cross found by the doorway of the Abbey, all of which were pulverized, to the terrible conſternation of the island's inhabitants and believers worldwide. It was thought that the original St. John's Cross, located in the Infirmary in the rear of the abbey, was safe and sound, but when entering it to check on the cross, although ſtill present,

a priest discovered that it was covered in black polyamide—
furious, he started tearing the fabric from the cross, only to
realize that it was saturated in acid, and swiftly drawing his
wounded hands back and shouting *"Vade retro! Vade retro!"*
he watched as the cross dissolved before his eyes as if it was
wax melting in a furnace. Nearby in Glastonbury, close to the
summit of Wearyall Hill, a Holy Thorn tree, held to have
bloomed from the ground when St. Joseph of Arimathea
stuck his staff into it, was completely uprooted, nothing left
in its place, not even the roots of the tree, save for a gaping
void:

as onlookers pondered the abyss of the open ground and com-
miserated over the sacrilege, a breaking report was broadcast
over the radio stating that the Christ Redeemer statue at the
peak of Corcovado Mountain in Brazil had been completely
engulfed by poison ivy, the climbing vine having twisted
around the sculpture like a snake, winding and winding and
winding about it, covering the head and even the extended
arms, from which the vines dangled and stretched as if trying
to reach the very ground from which they erupted in order to
pull the sculpture to the center of the earth and bury it. When
the ivy was first removed, it was discovered that upon the left
arm of the Christ was written:

ART THOU THE CHRIST?

and upon the right arm:

APE IS US

but before either slogan could be removed the ivy regenerated
almost instantly, swiftly winding up and over the statue at
astonishing speeds, which made some of the faithful believe
that Satan was in fact in their midst, for, to them, nothing else
could explain the phenomena to which they were painful wit-
nesses, though other events were not as mystifying but still in
part bemusing, if not bizarre, like cryptic clues left by serial
killers, such as the 12 hand carved Pinocchio dolls that were
found hanging in the remains of the Hagia Sophia of Nicaea,
or Iznik, the global map of the ocean floor draped over the re-

mains of the Dura-Europos church in Syria, which in its leg-
end contained the statement, "Faith does not move mountains,
plate tectonics does," leading some authorities to entertain the
possibility that perhaps eco-terrorists were behind some of the
events, though, still, they could not come to a clear resolution
regarding that, or the 39 donkeys that were covered in oil and
dragging bundles of ziziphus trees behind them into Notre
Dame de Paris. While the earthquakes, famines, plagues, and
wars led many of the faithful to view the times as apocalyptic
despite the fact that such events occurred frequently throughout history, and while the attacks visited upon religious sites
the world over invoked a sense of fear among many believers,
it was however when swarms of churchgoers were found unconscious in houses of worship throughout Christendom that
mass fear started to take hold, leading many to stop attending church and to believe that perhaps the Lord had forsaken
them, that all of the events to which they were witness were
signs that there was no god, or that the Deists were right, that
He just started up the clock and took off for another galaxy
to start yet another species, or was just time traveling, despite
the fact that he was always already everywhere, but perhaps
the Deists were onto something, for if there was Auschwitz,
God could not exist, or so some argued, but was not the flood
worse than Auschwitz, and evidence that the Supreme Being
would willingly and without reservation destroy even the near
entirety of his own creation in a holocaust of water as if it
were as dispensable as a wafer? The void that opened beneath
the Holy Thorn tree in Glastonbury made many demoralized
believers think, "why not nothing instead of something," echoing

Origen's conviction that "the whole material creation is but the result of sin, its purpose is to serve as a purgatory, and it would have been much better if there never had been any need for it at all," and as they pondered and were mystified by such troubles, as that void entered into their bodies and they lost all sense of having any center, as the very circumference that they thought bounded and defined the universe seemed to be sucked into that void as if the center were but a black hole, in Circo Massimo, the troupe paraded around the stadium in states of pure merriment, for they had nearly finished another section of their sculpture, and were with their rifflers shaping and smoothing the entity beneath the foot, eliminating gouge marks and undulations in the surface, which once they ceased working was revealed to be the surface of an arachnid, in particular, the wandering spider, an aggressive and highly venomous beast the Portuguese referred to as armed, but it did not form the base of the sculpture, not even part of it; instead, the stone beneath it was pitched away as if to illustrate that, whatever the spider was, it was supported by nothing except itself, for its legs were all pointed directly beneath it as if it were trying to hold itself up on a single point, as if the crux that lent it stability was only itself, but this spider had no web in which to entrap others anymore.

After examining the base of the sculpture with delight and admiring the mastery with which the troupe executed it, how finely they cut oblivion beneath it, Triboulet and Aurora entered their ship-car and all followed suite, trailing alongside the vehicle as they paraded to the coast, the troupe leaping about in satyr and maenad costumes, with the sileni-like figures blowing upon their horns, clanging cymbals, banging tambours, and exulting as the animals accompanied them, with the monkeys hanging on the side of the ship-car and climbing over and around it, jumping onto its mast, or on top of the midgets, with some of the kids riding the goats, for they proved more tractable than the hyenas, who rushed close to the hull and leapt at its wheels and tried to bite them, or ran ahead of the ship-car as if leading the way as they laughed, while other kids frolicked about Triboulet and Aurora, and after shooting their coins around the floor of the vehicle, they came upon a crown and seizing it, ran to Aurora and placed it on her head. Ceremoniously lifting a flagon in the air, Triboulet toasted her, and after he removed the vessel from his lips, Aurora saw that they were glistening with the liquid; turning to taste it, she kissed him, and absorbed the honey on his fleshy upper lip, taking it into her pores, her veins trembling with desire as she bit him, drawing blood …

And so they journeyed till they reached Isola di Ponza, the destination Aurora had in mind, for as one who loved water and stone, she knew that Triboulet would relish its caves, grottoes, and beaches as well as that the whole island was a caldera rim of an extinct volcano whose rocky coast was composed of mostly kaolin and tuff. As Triboulet studied the layers of kaolinite and bentonite south of Scoglio Montagnello, Aurora unbraided her hair and dived into the Tyrrhenian, immersing herself in the brisk greenish-blue waters, her pores trembling and pulsing as they had never done so before, and Triboulet soon leapt after her, diving in and out of the water like a dolphin, finally following her into a grotto, where they swam both deeper into the earth and the darkness, but as they frolicked in the waters, the enigmatic attacks only intensified and there were fires about the world, all in relative close succession, imbuing each successive attack with extreme gravity, till it was absolutely clear that some radical politico-religious polemic was at hand, for on October 27 five effigies of Calvin were found burning in Geneva, and on October 31, an effigy of Luther was found burning in Eisleben, and then another was found in Wartburg, and yet still more, with effigies appearing in Coburg, Wittenberg, and Worms, while others it was reported continued to proliferate, incensing the religious community, with each now attacking the other, though the Calvinists, Lutherans, and Protestants united to oppose the Christians, whom they pledged once and for all to finally conquer, to level Christendom to the earth, for the reign of the Papacy had to come to an end, for all things end, even time itself, as all of them presumed, and so those united against the Christians felt as if triumph was to be in their hands and that it was only natural that the Christians had reigned for so long because they had not been *contra mundum* since Athanasius but were truly worldly people despite their pretensions to asceticism and spirituality—what they yearned and longed for and sustained was drama and worldly power, but their dominion over the earth would persist no longer and the papal bulls would be driven from Rome once and for all, killed by a great toreador in the arena before clowns, a conviction which they felt was confirmed by all of the mysterious acts at hand, though, despite each believer's unfailing faith, within every single one of them, there remained profound doubts, but few were honest enough to reveal such doubts and, since it was the third of its kind, all were deeply alarmed when they learned of the message burned into the façade of the Church of St. Peter in Antakya:

Ceci n'est pas un Christ

When Triboulet and Aurora emerged from the grotto, they gazed up at the rocks and saw the monkeys, hyenas, and goats poised on the cliffs, each perfectly still and silent, like emblems etched into the volcanic rim. Turning to Aurora, Triboulet removed his mask and she trembled and thought of the honey glistening on his lips and biting him once more, his blood washed over her lips and into the sea, dissipating in the water.

ADVENT

When the message burned into the façade of the Church of St. Peter in Antakya was discovered, the priests were horror-struck, but more so because after extinguishing the flames and dousing the façade with holy water, as the fire smoldered and petered out, suddenly, it burst into flame again, as if generated from the earth itself and despite continual attempts to extinguish it, the fire continued burning, an eternal flame, the cross and the simple but definitive refutation lighting up the night sky, which terrified the priests, causing them to wail and lament for they knew not what was to come. And although the effigies of Calvin and Luther were easy to extinguish, when the objects were investigated in close detail, the police announced that they were made of texts, Latin to be precise, and when scholars were brought in to assist the investigation, they explained that the effigies of Calvin were each constructed out of original copies of his *Institutio Christianæ Religionis*, and when they began reading the charred and moist remains of each effigy in order to determine if they contained further messages, or if they may have been composed of other texts as well, the head of one of the effigies cracked open, revealing a small white scroll that contained an image of three laughing babies, beneath whom was written the phrase:

SUMMA TURPITUDINE ABOMINATIO EST

It was soon confirmed, too, that further effigies of Luther were found burning in different significant sites throughout Europe; in fact, a total of 95 effigies were reported and after they were examined, it was announced that, just as with the

Calvin effigies, the Luther effigies were also made of texts,
which, once deciphered, scholars explained to be a composite
of original editions of Luther's Bible, his hymns, and his cel-
ebrated theses, while on All Hallows Eve, the same day that
the effigies of Luther were found burning, a long scroll titled
THESES NOVA was nailed to one of the doors of St. Peter's
Basilica by someone in a festive costume, though the Cara-
binieri were not sure whether it was an actual jester, someone
in a Punchinello costume, or someone impersonating one of
the Pontifical Swiss guards, for the costumes of each were all
quite similar, but in the All Hallows melee the culprit could
not be apprehended. The document was signed *Chess Jurist
& the Drastic Ouijas*, which led some members of the Euro-
pean Bureau of Investigation to presume that a black magic
cult was responsible for penning the manifesto while others,
including papal authorities, were skeptical and refused to give
a definitive response before studying the scroll in more detail.
Whether it was nailed by someone connected with the organization responsible for the other incidents throughout the
world had also yet to be determined, but delegates from the
United Nations and the Great Sovereign Body of the Joint
Chiefs of Staff of the U.S. Government were now certain that
there was in fact one organization orchestrating the attacks,
though they did not announce from where they believed it or
its members hailed, or what their ideology was, but simply
asserted that it was an anti-clerical if not anti-monarchal terrorist faction of some kind, possibly including radical leftist
academics, or aesthetico-atheist extremists, for their messages
were too clever and witty to be the work of mere anarchists, let

alone radical Islamic sects; also, they indicated a sophisticated
knowledge of the history of religion, aesthetics, and mythol-
ogy as well as an astute knowledge of multiple languages. According to papal authorities, there were less than 10 scholars
capable of composing sentences with perfect grammar as
complex as those contained in what they were calling the "Aramaic fabric" and each of them had been extensively interro-
gated, and, it was rumored, even tortured, but all to no avail,
which left the author(s) of the fabric a mystery and the Papacy
inordinately vexed. If the renewed and continual acts of often
cryptic vandalism not only profoundly concerned but further
incensed the Papacy, they made clear to them that, despite
the fact that not one person had been harmed in any of the
incidents, a political campaign as vehement as the one enacted
against Christendom during the French Revolution had commenced, which they were especially convinced of when they
learnt that on 10 November, not only did another 39 donkeys
saturated in oil dragging bundles of ziziphus trees behind
them trot into Notre Dame de Paris, but as parishioners and
clergymen struggled to push and drag out of the church the
"obstinate and obscene animals," who not only destroyed many
sacred objects when defending themselves against their at-
tackers, kicking their hind legs as fiercely as they struck with
their front hooves and bit, above the doorway to the Gothic
cathedral, a sign was affixed that contained a slogan distinctly
similar to one used during the dechristianization campaign.
Due to the uproar caused by the donkeys, between their braying, everyone's shouts, and the din of their tramping around
and smashing things, no one heard or saw the culprits, and the

sign was not discovered until later, after a disturbing incident that occurred with one of the priests. While the debris was being cleaned up, which included not only damaged sacred relics but bounteous stacks of feces left behind by the beasts during their near stampede, as well as copious masses of semen, it started to rain, which made the donkeys rush towards the cathedral to edge their way back into it and as they were being forced out again, it was noticed that there were brands on more than half of the donkey's buttocks, but when they were examined more closely, it was observed that, although some letters repeated, only two pairs of donkeys had the same two letters in the same order on their buttocks:

NA HI RA TE ON PH AT MP IO LA

IS LA TÉ LI OS ET IL DE OP L'I RR LE

yet, of the second pair, one of them contained an apostrophe, though it was hard to see because it was on the ridge of the crack of the donkey's ass, but while those two donkey's buttocks were nearly identical, there was a slight variation between them, yet since the markings on the buttocks of all of the other donkeys were different, it was ruled out that they were actually brands, though each donkey could have belonged to a different owner, but that possibility was rejected since brands aren't generally made on that part of the buttock while they also often contain a pictorial symbol, and as the mystery of the donkey's buttocks was being pondered, a make-shift barn was constructed to corral the animals, which had to be secured as evidence, though, whether the Police Nationale would house the donkeys in one of their stations remained to be determined, for feeding donkeys is *"très très cher,"* so the French authorities ceaselessly ruminated over the fate of the donkeys as if trying to solve a riddle, for they delighted in hermeneutical puzzles, and they thought out every possible solution, *"mais,"* protested the priests, *"les bêtes doivent être détenus!"* When the donkeys finally herded into the make-shift barn and gathered around the barley straw left to pacify them, one of the priests, who had a particular affection for donkeys, watched them as they were feeding; in gazing continually at the animals, he couldn't help but stare at their buttocks, for that was all he could see, and since he was so prone to making exegeses of complex texts, he was attracted to the significatory system displayed before him and prompted to engage in a semiotic evaluation of it, but soon realized that it didn't require analysis per se, simply rearrangement, but instead of mentally rearranging the letters, he decided to try to actually shift the donkeys around, particularly because of his fondness for the animals, whom he enjoyed touching, so he struggled with the beasts of burden, some of whom obeyed him, others whom did not, and as he attempted to rearrange them and form words with the asses of the asses, it came to him at last what the letters spelt out. Elated, although he knew he was correct, despite the fact that they were part of the scene of the crime, he begin feverishly whipping the asses with one of the ziziphus branches to get them into place because he wanted to physically spell out the phrase with the ass tablets; as they started to move, he became more and more ecstatic when, at last, although one letter was missing, he finally spelled out the phrase with the fleshy tablets themselves, exulting when he recited it aloud, for his exegetical skills truly pleased him:

TE MP LE DE LA RA IS ON

L'I RR AT IO NA LI TÉ ET LA PH IL OS OP HI

Everyone was astonished by his rapturous ejaculation, for why would a priest exult about reason, irrationality, and philosophy? Or rather, see such as temples? When the parishioners and his fellow clergymen rushed outside to investigate the clamor, they saw him clinging to one of the donkey's necks and pointing to the sign above the doorway of the cathedral and shouting: *"Asses! O ânes impies!"* after which he fell to the ground, a demented, maniacal grin stretching across his face as he perished in a state of retarded ecstasy. While convincing them that a politico-religious campaign of some kind was in fact in operation, this quite serious but absurd, bizarre event completely incensed the Papacy, which asserted that it would not stand for such mockery, though, as an esoteric faction of believers argued: "It could very well have been an act of God, for, although His ways are mysterious, they are not contradictory—since the supernatural is irrational, He might very well take the form of a donkey, because, as logic proves, unlike a squared circle, a donkey is not a contradiction—*non includit contradictionem, Deum assumere naturam asininam.*"

Although the 12 effigies of Pinocchio found hanging in the
Hagia Sophia of Nicaea were hardly as blasphemous, what
they intended to convey was clear, and although seemingly innocuous, if not frivolous and forgettable, a mere sophomoric
gesture of little significance that the church would soon vomit
forth like a lukewarm sinner, the frivolity of the message hardly
detracted from its intent. Something however transformed the
gesture from the frivolous to the wounding and made it sting
and burn more even than the desecration of the Christ Pantocrator in Jerusalem. When the Pinocchio effigies were examined, it was discovered that, just as with the donkeys, they too
contained a series of letters that formed a code, though each
individual significatory symbol was not branded on the different puppet's buttocks. Unlike most if not all puppets, these
were not only anatomically correct but enlivened—the letters
were found on each effigy's genitals, with one letter on each
testicle and another on its erect cock. In total, there were 34
letters and one exclamation point, making for nearly 200,000
possible configurations, and the priests were benumbed by
the absurd task of deciphering the code, for most of the configurations were completely senseless, though, even what was
considered senseless might contain a clue, so they could not
discount any configuration, therefore they catalogued every
one of them, diligently studying each nonsensical anagram,
which, despite their using a computerized anagram generator,
remained a laborious undertaking, and as they continued day
after night after day after night after week upon week upon
week, the generally ludicrous phrases coupled with the priests'
anxiety and insomnia produced in them states of near-demen-

tia, leading to their frequently bursting into fits of uncontrollable laughter, especially when one of them tried to convince
the others that the anagram *"A Ladybug Innermost!"* was the
clue that they were looking for yet, despite its symbolic connec-
tion to the Virgin Mary, the other priests were not convinced,
especially since none of the sacrilegious acts referenced her,
nor were any acts of vandalism committed against icons of her,
so they persisted, almost convulsively giggling when coming
upon configurations such as *"My a broadening lust!"*, *"A banned
orgy litmus!"*, and *"A bayed morning lust!"*, while others such
as *"A drum beat singly on!"* and *"A brayed molting sun!"* were,
they thought, perhaps the phrases that they were searching
for, though they still needed to be deciphered, but they eventually abandoned those phrases, for after spending two days
trying to interpret them, three of the priests started shaking
violently, their bodies overcome with tremors as they were
seized by uncontrollable bursts of laughter and then finally
died, one of them exclaiming just before he perished, *"The
Virgin Mary is not a la-dy bug …"*

    After autopsies were performed on the three priests,
the pathologist discovered that each of them suffered from
kuru, an incurable degenerative neurological disorder commonly known as "laughing sickness." Since the said priests
had been missionaries and spent time amongst the Fore
tribe of Papua New Guinea, it was believed that during their
tenure there they must have consumed human flesh, though,
unknowingly of course, for while they were accustomed
to digesting unleavened bread, they were clearly not accustomed to digesting Papua New Guineans, despite their being

especially savory—such are the perils of being a missionary, though some members of the press found their deaths an act of poetic justice … When the remaining priests came upon the configuration "*Banned soma liturgy!*", due to its implied positive valuation of matter, it seemed to contain pagan resonances, but, after much deliberation, that hypothesis was abandoned and they concluded that the two sets of six effigies formed the same message, which they narrowed down to two phrases: one which had a clear religious tonality, and another which they found of no consequence at all, but which still seemed to them possibly significant:

A Banding Yule Storm!
Made in Glastonbury!

When conferring with officials at the Vatican, the priests soon realized that the message was in fact of considerable magnitude and suffused with terrible moral gravity, for it meant that the Pinocchio effigies were carved from the wood of the tree that sprung from the staff of Joseph of Arimathea. Far from frivolous or sophomoric, it was indeed malevolent, if not "an act of outright evil," which led the Papacy to claim that they were quite possibly contending with Satan himself and his earthly representatives. How else explain that none of the culprits were ever apprehended? And how else explain such parodic blasphemy except by attributing the acts to some satanic jester? When a scroll with passages from Celsus's *True Word* was found issuing as if from the wound of Christ in the statue atop the peak of the *Archibasilica Sanctissimi*

Salvatoris, invoking St. Augustine and Aquinas, the Vatican declared that, lest anyone be deceived, they would not turn the other cheek to such acts.

"While the sharp sword in Christ's mouth is symbolic of His authoritative word of command which destroys the earth's armies by divine power, those armies will be killed by Christ's sword, and the number of the dead will be so great that the vultures will not be able to consume them all. Liberal pacifists and other weekender Christians, all of whom have turned the Bible into a New Age Chinese menu, may wish to emphasize God's love, but the Lord is wrathful, too—even the most seemingly faithful and upright men are cast out by God. Alas, if only all believers were like Pascal and Kierkegaard!

O, the verdicts against the wicked are fierce and the second coming of the Christ will bring on worldwide judgment unparalleled in Scripture since the time of Noah's flood." The pope then proclaimed that, while hesitant to endow the phrase "A Banding Yule Storm!" with any definite meaning, all of the events signaled to him "the onset of a war and under such circumstances, a *bellum justum* if entirely warranted," and, if necessary, which was quite probable, and which they seemed hungry to invoke, they may very well start "a *bellum sacrum*."

Returning from Isola di Ponza, where Triboulet remained to savor his solitude and continue examining the geological stratifications of the island, Aurora sent the troupe to Piazza del Popolo to prepare for his return as the Vatican was fomenting storms of hell-fire and threatening the world with war and worse, Judgment Day prognostications. Dressing the open square before sunrise, the troupe hung large blue streamers with rose bunting from all of the surrounding buildings as well as along Via Cola di Rienzo, Via Conciliazione, and Via del Corso. Then, returning to the piazza, they constructed intricate stage sets of the inferno, which included each of its different circles, a foreboding gate near which a boat lay close by, a City of Dis, its obligatory Stygian marsh, Malebolge (complete with all of its *Bolgie*), and even the reputed icy lake with a beautiful multi-colored effigy of Satan. Above the whole display was a silk map of the inferno; in addition, directly in front of it, a seating arrangement had been made for select members of the troupe, who were dressed as different biblical figures, including Cain, who was rather uncomfortably situated on a plow, Abel, whose seat of a milk-pail was a bit more comfortable but still not so pleasant, Noah, who, also rather uncomfortably, was sitting on his ark, while Japheth was splayed out on tiles, Isaac on an altar, Lot on the edge of a door, his wife on an ever dwindling pile of salt, Jacob on a stone, Benjamin on a sack, the Pharaoh on a pile of sand, Samson on a column, James on a net, Rachel on a pack, and Job on a heap of dung.

As a cock crowed signaling the rising of the sun, in the bright morning hours, costumed as the various people, animals, and monsters of the inferno, to the blast of *salpinxes* and the thunderous clamor of drums and cymbals, while the citizens of Rome flooded into the piazza, the troupe enacted scenes from the different circles, which began with a man in a purple vestment crying out, "I'm lost, I'm lost, I can't find the one true way," to which some in the piazza replied, offering him consolation, "You will find it," while others contested: There is no one true way, to which he pleaded, "I want the straight path!" which everyone in the troupe contested, affirming: There is no straight path; all truth is crooked; time itself is a circle! while people from the crowd encouraged, "There's no way to get lost—all roads lead to Rome!" which others disputed, rejoinding: There's no way; get lost—each road leads to a different place! and confusedly he walked on, only to be accosted by the three aged women, who appeared in the guise of a lion, leopard, and she-wolf, and as the last lunged toward him, her wrinkled breasts dangling in the air like insults, he fled to a *basso loco* and came upon Aurora, costumed as Virgil, and she took him by the arm as they approached the foreboding gate, above which was written

Lasciate ogne ragione, voi ch'intrate

and beside which were many of Triboulet's hyenas, and as Aurora entered the gate with her guest, who thought she looked hauntingly familiar, the hyenas began laughing, prompted by the monkeys, who leapt over and around the gate, swinging from it with glee, for it was such a perfect object from which to swing. At that moment, although the performance had already begun, Paul, Esau, Moses, Adam and Eve, Matthew, and Peter arrived, all demanding seats, but, as usual, Jesus neglected to appear. As the troupe sought to accommodate the late-comers while the crowd boisterously objected, Paul waited patiently, but Esau grumbled, especially when Adam was given a seat in the middle of the gathering, but more so when Eve sat on Adam's lap instead of his, though not before placing a bundle of fig leafs upon his crotch. A bench was found for

Matthew and an armchair for Peter, but Moses had to sit on the outskirts with the bleating goats. Continuing on, as various members of the troupe leapt around and spit fire from their mouths, the lost man and her guide were ferried over a pestiferous river, but only after offering the boatman *guanciale, mozzarella di bufala*, and *polpo*, though he didn't of course eat all of those gifts at once, which would have been repugnant, something that would disturb his sense of taste; he just wanted to stock up for, as he said, "it's hard to get such foods down here," but as they walked onward, despite the fact that it was only morning, they wished they had kept some of the *guanciale*, for when they came upon Homer, Horace, Ovid, and Penthesilea they were so honored that they wanted to offer some of it to each of them, but instead, all they could share with them was biscotti, and since it had been so long since Orpheus had partaken of the cookie, despite the fact that his ceaseless lyre playing irritated Cicero, the magnanimous orator broke a piece of his biscotti and handing it to the poet said, "Take this and eat it," and it so delighted Orpheus that, to the great consternation of Cicero, he could not help but begin playing upon his lyre again and while the lost one and his guide were enchanted by Orpheus's music, as too were the babies covered in soil that they found sitting around the circle, they came upon Minos, who was portrayed by a monkey, but since he didn't have a tail, he was wrapping a sinuous branch around himself to indicate which circle each sinner should go to and as he pointed to different people in the crowd commanding each to go to this or that circle, many in the troupe objected, protesting: I'm more heretical than treacherous!

I don't belong in a lower circle! while people in the crowd asked, "What if you're equally lustful and greedy, where do you go?" which made some wonder if it's possible to travel from circle to circle, or if one is sent from circle to circle, while others believed some in higher circles belonged in lower circles, and still others questioned the very validity of the punishments as those in the different circles shouted from set to set to set. First they heard the voice of Semiramis, who asserted, "If lechery is always determined, there is no actual volition. Set me free!" but it was difficult to hear her over the shouts of the many priests and preachers and popes—who were portrayed by monkeys—in her circle, and despite their beliefs, they shouted in unison, wanting to affirm Semiramis's view for, if it were true, it would release them from the circle, too, just as they sought to affirm the view of all of those in the third circle, who argued, "If there is *volonté générale*, then we're innocent! It's not our will that we follow, but the will of the people which drives us!" and Triboulet's goats, who wandered throughout the piazza, began fornicating next to Moses, who, gazing upon his tablets, sought to find a law with which he could make the goats cease their acts, but there was no prohibition against animal fornication, so Moses prayed to God to rid him of God and make him a Kantian, and as the goats continued screwing with ever greater and greater intensity and pleasure, Moses grew so perturbed that he dropped his tablets, which made many exult, and those in the third circle triumphantly avowed, "Now we're definitely innocent!" to which those in the fourth circle riposted, avowing that "everything is an act of will— there are no accidents!" which made some believers question

whether or not Moses actually intended to deliberately shatter
the tablets and as the lost man and his guide proceeded onward, accompanied by the raucous sound of the ecstasy of the
goats, who someone shouted were "just being driven by the
will of the entirety of goats" so they could not be held account-
able for their screwing, the troupe members continued to spit
fire from their mouths like volcanic geysers, and the two wanderers came to the swamp-like water of the river Styx, and
those gurgling just beneath its pestilential surface murmured,
their faces grim, stern, and dour, "It's only through the body
that we can know the *Ding-an-sich*. But there is no freedom,
for we are ruled by necessity and nothing can change our con-
duct, so we must be set free to exult in our nihilism! Do you
not love resignation?" Finding this inordinately humorous,
Aurora herself turned to the crowd assembled in the piazza
and proclaimed: If you wanna know the *Ding-an-sich*, get your
head outta your ass and get to the Hadron Collider! *Ding,
ding, ding!* The limits of consciousness were reached in the
19th century! which provoked great peals of laughter amongst
some, and as the gurgling waters of the Styx bubbled and
bubbled, which was actually an enormous vat of *acquacotta*,
the lost man and his guide continued further into the remaining circles while members of the troupe passed out bowls of
the soup and threw everyone bits of *guanciale*, which the
monkeys tried to grab, running around the piazza, screeching
and hooing, at which point the sixth circle was reached, yet
when the beasts did finally acquire some of the unsmoked
bacon, they were so pleased by the sight of Epicurus that they
brought him their bits of meat, and as he held one of the mon-

keys in his arms and consumed the bacon, relishing its delicate texture, he affirmed that, "although some may view me as a heretic, it is true that the soul dies with the body, and there is no rational cause for fear," at which point the three aged women, who were now costumed as Furies, their skin painted black, their hair undulating with snakes, rose up and hissed and howled and rent their breasts, striking themselves and shrieking, spitting black foam from their mouths as blood dripped from their nipples, wailing that "the End is nigh, the Time is near, the Day of Days is upon us—He is coming with the sword! Fire! Damnation! Eternal punishment! *Bellum justum; bellum sacrum!*" but Epicurus only laughed at their grotesque fulminations, especially when seeing the quizzical manner with which the monkeys gazed at them, which amused Aurora as well, who, turning to the crowd, went beyond Epicurus when proclaiming: Bodies we are through and through, and nothing besides; and soul is merely a word for something about the body, which made the Furies beat their breasts with even greater wrath, and many found the sight of the three aged women with blackened skin foaming and fulminating grotesque; laughing, as they were finishing their *acquacotta*, the crowd spit chewed bits of *guanciale* at them; as the Furies retrieved the remnants and shoved them into their mouths, suddenly, the Minotaur appeared, and the lost one recoiled in fear while his guide was full of awe and her limbs pulsed with a myriad of electrifying sensations as she thought of that decisive moment in the labyrinth. Standing before a river of boiling blood and fire—which was actually grappa surrounded by coils of dry ice—the Minotaur began to snort and groan and

149

pace around Aurora and the lost man while someone from
another circle shouted, "we cannot but will what is an unqualified good," prompting members of the troupe to rejoin: There
is no unqualified good! while still another pointed at his watch
and pontificated with unswerving authority about "the permanent timeliness of universal moral law," to which other members of the troupe countered: Can you give yourself your own
evil and your own good, and hang your will over yourself as
a law? as centaurs leapt upwards as if trying to overcome
gravity, and as the lost one continued to flee from the Minotaur, harpies and ferocious dogs—once again costumed
members of the troupe—bandied about the City of Dis and,
despite it still being very early, the grappa was distributed
throughout the piazza to the immense pleasure of those
present while the midgets kept spitting fire into the air as the
lost one coursed through the rest of the circles with his guide,
who was chased by the Minotaur while a troupe member
dressed as Ficino exulted about the delight of sodomy, arguing that, "if it is so pleasurable, how could it be against nature,
for if nature did not endow us with prostates, then God did,
and friction causes heat, and boils the blood, and any priest
will tell you that, as will many popes, though they can't stop
thinking about their semen instead of thinking of themselves
as semen," and gulping down the grappa, everyone rejoiced
and called for more as the lost one and his guide continued
even further while the Minotaur fervently pursued them and
when reaching the absolute midpoint of the final circle, in
the very center of Cocytus, the infamous beast of Crete devoured the lost one, tore him limb from limb, till there was

nothing left of him but bones, and as the Minotaur whispered to the crowd: The world is will to power—and nothing besides. And you yourselves are this will to power—and
nothing besides! Do not be deceived by the lie of the altru-
ists—they too want power! the troupe took up the lost one's
bones and drumming with them on the pavement of Piazza
del Popolo, they beat a slow, strong, steady rhythm as the set
pieces of each circle were collapsed—as one was piled on top
of another, the drummers punctuated the collapsing with
their kick drums and a crash of cymbals, and after all of the
circles were collected, the foreboding gate, Charon's boat, the
City of Dis, the Stygian marsh, Malebolge and each of its
Bolgie were then thrown on top of Cocytus as the torches
surrounding the piazza were each blown out, and the beautiful multi-colored effigy of Satan was dragged into the center
of the piazza and dressed in the robes of death and paraded
around with a sickle, though, unlike the traditional image of
death, this one had a protruding belly, an enormous nose,
and a hump—it resembled some malformed beast which,
due to its grotesqueness, was found extraordinarily comical,
and thinking it was a piñata, the kids came running into the
piazza with sticks and started beating the effigy, and then the
hyenas joined in the melee and leapt at it too, tearing it to
pieces, as did the goats, which incited those in the piazza to
run forward and join in tearing the effigy, until, at last, it
burst into pieces, with *salsiccia, casu marzu, barbozzo, budel-
lacci, lampone, braciole di maiale, osso buco,* olives, fruits, and
sundry other treats flowing out of it in every direction, which
goaded the troupe into sounding all their instruments, pro-

ducing an incredible cacophony, which they sustained for minutes and minutes and minutes.

Removing her Virgil costume, Aurora stood at the southernmost end of the piazza and, taking up her bow, assumed an open stance, then aimed at the map of the inferno hanging above the effigy of Satan, closed her eyes, grounded her bow, placed and nocked the arrow and raising it, deftly drew back the string then forthwith let the arrow sail——cutting through the air, but perfectly still, everyone watched in awe as, swiftly, the arrow flew to the exact center of its target and cut through it, but dragged it further on to the northernmost end of the piazza, where hung a map of the cosmos, and plunged it into its next mark, which was a black hole, as the sound of a cock crowing was heard in the distance.

Lowering her bow and opening her eyes, Aurora raised her hands in the air in a circular movement and, turning about, proceeded through a series of sinuous movements, complete with daedalic evolutions, which wound and unwound like the ecliptic. Turning to the crowd that had gathered before her, with a piercing shout she proclaimed:

The time to celebrate has indeed come, but before we can commence, yet another task remains ...

Picking up her bow, she shot an arrow towards the far end of the piazza, directing everyone's attention to the Furies, who had escaped the inferno and, unbeknownst to the celebrants, were circling about them, spitting black foam from their mouths, casting pitch at the earth, defecating violently, and defaming matter and all earthly things as they brandished

their torches, waving them through the air like weapons, calling hell-fire upon the world. Turning about three times, they
hissed at the crowd, squirt blood from their nipples, and threw
snakes at them, to which the crowd retaliated by grabbing tomatoes from the exploded body of the Satan-Death effigy and
pelting the Furies with them, who only laughed and smeared
the remnants over their blackened bodies, the seeds sticking to
them like leeches. Flummoxed, the crowd grabbed more veg-
etables and pelted the figures with them, then threw sausages
at them, olives, onions, and garlic, thinking that, perhaps, at
very least, as with vampires, the latter would dispel them, but
the Furies devoured whatever was cast at them, especially the
casu marzu, sometimes even stuffing the different foods into
their hollows and then shrieking,

"Only man defecates — angels
have no orifices! Repent, impure ones! Cast away your flesh,
or we will devour you on the final day, tear you limb from limb,
decimate you worse than any
Minotaur! Repent!" Spitting into their torches, ever greater and
hotter flames shot from them towards the crowd, and the Furies
began to stamp their feet and approach the crowd, for it was losing its determination, and as the
bestial ones cast pitch at the crowd
and squirted more blood at them,
which streamed from their breasts
like acid rain, the Furies barked:
"All is vanity and vexation of
spirit! Laughter is mad: and of
mirth, What doeth it?

The dead are to be praiſed more than thee!" And cloſing in upon the crowd, the Furieſ began weaving a circle around them aſ if drawing an ever tightening web that would conſtrict all within it, and aſ they were about to finiſh their deed and ſtrangle all of the revelerſ, they fumed: "Even childhood and youth are vanity! Vanity of vanitieſ, all iſ vanity!" and the kidſ jolted forward from every portico, crevice, ſtreet, and pathway and ſurrounded the furiouſ croneſ and ſtarted piſſing on them, ſcowling and ſhrieking aſ they ſprayed them with their urine, veritably ſaturating the aged beaſtſ aſ if they had barrelſ of piſſ to diſcharge, and all watched in aſtoniſhment aſ their voluminouſ egeſta made the plaited ſnare of the croneſ diſſolve,

ſtirring the troupe to sound their double flutes and clang their cymbals as the old women began to wither and everyone surrounded them and taking heaps of soil which the troupe had placed in pails around the piazza in case the inferno actually caught fire, ſtarted to cleanse the Furies, rubbing the *solum* over their arms, breaſts, ſtomachs, backs, and buttocks, after which they carried the aged women to the fountains at the north end of the piazza and plunging them into the brisk water, washed the soil from their bodies, then covered the ground with animal skins and laid the aged ones down, rubbed their bodies with oils and dressed them anew. They were old but radiant, their youthful ſplendor ſtill present in their beautifully wrinkled skin, for they welcomed the natural decay of their bodies and never altered their flesh, and Triboulet loved and reſpected their fragility.

And though there was a great revel, and the troupe performed more raucously than ever, and everyone feaſted, while those in the crowd seemed to be ſtrengthened by the transmogrification of the Furies and the parody of the inferno, which lessened their fear, many others remained anxious, for the intensity with which the Papacy and the preachers and priests assured the world that the end was nigh was unsettling, and the famines and earthquakes and wars swayed even the lukewarm who thought aloud, "why risk eternal punishment, why not simply take the wager and obey," for the wrathful storms truly terrified them.

Hearing such frets, and smelling the fear that fed them, provoking them to possibly capitulate, Aurora secured her bow to her back, took up two torches even though it was still daylight, lit them, and then proceeded to wander around the piazza whispering something, the eyes behind her mask stern and focused, and as she continued wandering, other members of the troupe also picked up torches, with each lighting the other's torch, passing the flame from one torch to another as they circled and circled the enormous piazza, suffused with a terrible solemnity, each of them whispering in different tongues, running up to passersby and pleading, till their voices began to rise in volume, a *sotto voce* chorus echoing across the piazza as the sound of another cock crowing was heard:

" אני מחפש את אלוהים ! אני מחפש את אלוהים ! "

"Cerco Dio! Cerco Dio!"

" أعوذ بالله ! أعوذ بالله ! "

and as they continued to cry out incessantly in each different tongue, "I seek God! I seek God!" their voices in crescendo, tongue and tongue clashing, the piazza was full not only of Romans, but tourists from throughout the world, some laughing, some shouting, some mocking, some questioning, others objurgating:

Has he got lost?

Which god are you looking for?

Is he afraid of us?

Did he go to China? Emigrate to another galaxy?

"Just put a coin in the coffer!"

Did he lose his way like a child? Or is he hiding?

No, he's at Sant'Eustachio drinking espresso & waiting for Placidus to appear!

"Just take the wager!"

The odds of the wager are amiss—it's not a fifty-fifty bet! What if YHVH awaits, or Ahura Mazda, or Gitche Manitou? Or?—

Is it God who created man, or man who created God?

"*Repent!*"

Jumping into their midst, Aurora pierced them with her eyes and brandishing her torches aloft she cried: The prophets speak to you of end times and of cataclysms and call for you to repent, denouncing Triboulet and our troupe as 'the devil's brethren,' and they interpret the natural violence of the earth as signs of an apocalypse, but the earth has been in such tumult for billions of years. E x t e n d your knowledge of time—*study geology, not theology!* It is one thing for God to sacrifice his son for the sake of mankind, leaving him to cry out, '*Eli, Eli, lama sabachthani?*' but it is another to permit the sacrifice of millions—if there is an Auschwitz, can there be a God? If there is a Khmer Rouge, can there be a God? If there is a Rwanda, can there be a God? If there is —.

And if there is, is He who permits such events worthy of veneration? They tell you the Christ is coming and that the end time is nigh, but is not the destruction that we have witnessed a sign that … *God is dead?* That *we have killed him*—you and I! That all of us are his murderers. That we *had* to murder him? The prophets and preachers and theorists all proclaim that it is not so, that the proclamation of the death of God was presumptuous, as this faith-rich age testifies! But it is not true—the earth does move! Where is God? He is dead, the smell of his decomposing body surrounds us, and it is his shadow alone which lives on, echoing through time like a pale ghost—*that* is what the people witness, not a faith-rich age but a tremendous, gruesome, decaying shadow that hovers over us like a specter, festering within the cavities of our flesh, living on in those too weak to face the meaninglessness of the cosmos and to create *their own* meaning, O life-impoverished ones! It is only due to the ways of humans that the shadow is still shown on cave walls, and may be for thousands of years, but it is only a shadow, yet one that must be vanquished, too! Let us affirm the mortal conditions of existence! Death is not to be feared but welcomed. It is the very culmination of existence. Without one, the other does not exist; the unwinding of one is the winding of the other. But soul—that is just a word! Let us commence with festivals, and with games! Let laughter reign!

Although many were emboldened by Aurora's thoughts, others were struck as if with a great sickness and mourned and wailed as if having lost a child, wandering about in veils they drew over themselves from head to foot, and she approached them and greeted them anew and sought to tend them, but when she offered them her nectar, they refused, and when she offered them fine foods, they refused, and when she danced for them, they turned their backs. Lending full expression to their grief, they abstained from word, gesture, stopped moving altogether; became stony, plagued.

When the three aged women came forward after Aurora called to them, she whispered to them in private; after they finished conversing, the aged women went to the ship-car, gathered some things, then eventually stood before the grief-stricken mourners and, after attempting to assuage their grief but to no avail, they formed a pyramid in front of the stony figures.

The first aged woman exposed herself to them, displaying her genitals, laying bare what is veiled, for she had made them neat and smooth as a little boy's skin.

Immediately thereafter, the second aged woman pulled up her skirt from the bottom and exposed to sight her genitals, agitating them with her hands, molding the flesh into the shape of a little child, which she then caressed and gently manipulated.

Finally, the third aged woman, who was at the top of the pyramid, lifted up her gown, revealed her uncomely womb, and behold! there was the child Triboulet laughing inside her.

As the stony figures gazed upon the childlike pubis of the first woman, feasted on the comical display of the next, then upon the extraordinary sight of the last, their grief began to swiftly dissipate, but it was when the doorless, unrestrained spectacle of the three aged women's genitals were through a video projection system magnified and displayed upon all of the surrounding buildings, including upon the old churches of the piazza, that they finally erupted into wild peals of laughter, for through digital manipulation, the heads, bellies, and genitals of the three aged women were all united and resembled some grotesque figurine and the stony ones were immediately put at ease, their nausea dissipated, and they joyfully took up the nectar that Aurora brought to them and drank it as if ravenous, watching the flickering images flash from building to building.

While the troupe & *alia* were in the midst of their celebrations, a cote of Pontifical Swiss guards stormed into the piazza and seized Aurora, the three aged women, and Triboulet, who, unbeknownst to everyone present, was disguised as the Minotaur. When the guards went to catch him, he did not move, but willingly held out his hands and, laughing, invited them to bind him and lead him away, which they found unsettling, feeling almost ashamed that they were arresting him, though they were not sure why and were assuaged by the fact that they were only fulfilling their papal obligation.

In the prison below the Vatican, which had been defunct for over 60 years, Aurora and the three aged women were separated from Triboulet, who was placed in a cell far from theirs, his hands tightly bound behind his back. Once the pope, several cardinals, bishops, and one of the Pontifical Councils gathered in a room above the prison, Triboulet, who was still costumed as a Minotaur, was brought before them.

"Let him stand free; he will not escape now."

After the guards unbound Triboulet, he bowed to those before him, expressing his gratitude for their lenience; finding a hint of mockery in his salutation, the pope did not return it and proceeded sternly with his inquiry.

"We know that you are commonly addressed with the pseudonym Triboulet, but—*what is your orthonym?*"

Reaching into his coſtume, Triboulet removed his wooden blocks and began juggling, to which the pope vehemently proteſted.

"We will not ſtand for this impertinence! Put down those toys and reveal your orthonym at once."

Triboulet did not cease tossing his blocks, but threw them higher and higher into the air, manipulating them with great velocity and variation for, juſt as when he juggled them on the Appia Antica when firſt arriving in Rome, he was ſpelling something with the blocks, ſpelling exaᴄtly what he ſpelt out that day as the blocks h o v e r e d momentarily in the air, but although the pope and his cortege were watching Triboulet closely, he realized that they were not observing the words that he was forming, for they devoted attention ſtriᴄtly to the grave and solemn since that was what they believed was the only thing of significance, and so, one by one, he tossed the blocks on the ground, each of them ſtriking the purple tiled floor like a dagger:

I

AM

HE

WHO

YOU

THOUGHT

WAS HE

BUT I AM NO LONGER

HE

As each block struck the floor, more & more members of the pope's cortege rose, and once they saw what he was spelling out, all of them stood up, though, at first, it wasn't clear whether they were merely admiring how adept a carney he was, or whether they were astonished by the cryptic answer he was writing, as if with his finger in the ground, and the shape that he formed with the letters.

Astounded, the pope commanded the guards to remove the Minotaur mask from Triboulet's head, but it did not reveal the entirety of his face, for beneath it he was wearing another mask, the one he had donned since arriving in Rome. Incensed, the pope shook his Pastoral staff in the air and commanded Triboulet to reveal his identity at once.

I am excruciatingly near yet I am completely absent.

"Strip that mask from his face!"

Tentatively, the guards approached Triboulet, though, they did not know why, full of trembling. Turning towards them, Triboulet opened his arms in a conciliatory manner and lowered his head so as to ease the removal of the mask. Once they stripped him of the disguise, they retreated and the pope and his cortege watched as Triboulet slowly raised his head, his long, shoulder-length hair covering his face till he parted his hair and his eyes came into direct contact with theirs— gazing upon his full visage for the first time, they shuddered, some of them falling to their knees, others fainting, one of the cardinals even convulsing, vomiting.

Banging his staff on the ground, the pope turned to the guards and barked, "Remove his clothes!"

Refusing his command, the guards laid down their swords and prostrated themselves before Triboulet, who laughed.

"I command you to strip him or you will be stripped of your stations. *Do you know who you prostrate yourselves before?* Remember, many will come claiming His name, and many will be misled. Are you deceived by physical resemblance alone? It is but another mask, the ruse of a trickster. Plastic surgery! Shape shifting! Strip him of that costume!"

Refusing to move, the guards prostrated themselves further, till their bodies were completely flush with the ground.

Rising, the pope approached Triboulet, accompanied by two bishops and a cardinal and, just as with the guards, Triboulet opened his arms in a conciliatory manner, surrendering his body to his interrogators, who removed the Minotaur costume. As he spread his arms out again they saw that not only were there wounds in the center of his hands, but there were wounds in his feet, and a wound in his side …

Stepping back in horror, the cardinal and one of the bishops were overcome; as their teeth chattered, the pope thrust Triboulet backwards with his staff, almost instinctively, or out of shock. While he continued examining Triboulet's body, the wounds started to bleed, which made the cardinal and the bishop fall to their knees, shuddering as they lowered themselves before him, only incensing the pope further, who stepped away from Triboulet to consult the council as the denuded one remained there, but perfectly without shame, his athletic body pulsing with strength, vigor, and sensuality.

As the hushed whispers of the pope and the council petered out, the vicar turned to Triboulet and asked, "Art thou the Christ?"

Reaching down, Triboulet seized a sword from one of
the Pontifical Guards, then lifted it in the air and tilting his
head back, gently lowered the sword into his mouth; holding
it within himself, he stretched out his arms and bowed, then
rose and removed the sword.

Shouting at the guards, who still lay prostrate before
him, the pope cursed, "And you think that this is the Christ?
Take him to the cell! At once! *Sacrilege!*"

Although the Vicar of Christ remained skeptical, for the
stigmata could have been a parlor trick, some hysterical event,
or a group hallucination, he was still unsettled by the eerie if
not disturbing resemblance between Triboulet and the icons
of Christ, but physical resemblance alone was for him far from
sufficient for determining the identity of the savior. And if the
vicar was correct about whom he thought Triboulet actually
was, then the trickster could assume any form he wished. The
possibility of the stigmata being a mere group hallucination
was however ruled out by the fact that actual blood did fall from
Triboulet's wounds and stain the floor, though it may not have
been his own blood and instead that of an animal, or another
human, thus, samples of it were immediately brought to a lab
for analysis, but that still did not rule out the possibility of the
parlor trick, for if Triboulet was known for anything, it was
for acts of magic, and he was clearly a highly well-trained jester,
clown, or daredevil of some type, and his behavior was, to say
the least, not so Christian, though more radical priests, albeit
very few in number, saw his acts in part as *joca monachorum*,
but not entirely, for even the most ribald monks would not
go to the extents that he did, only, perhaps, Alcofribas Nasier.

Immediately after Triboulet was brought to his cell, the vicar and his council conferred over what just occurred then decided that the shroud of Turin should be flown to Rome at once—they anxiously awaited its arrival. During that interval, the vicar wanted to interrogate Aurora and the three aged women, but when they went to the cell to question them, the guards were absent, the women were gone, the doors were open, the fetters that had been around their feet lay strewn on the floor, and, most peculiar of all, a pile of old coins were scattered throughout the cell. At first, the vicar thought that the guards had been bribed by the women and he was ready to discipline them, but they were found unconscious elsewhere in the prison. When the vicar picked up a handful of the coins to examine them, he discovered to his astonishment that they seemed to be of no monetary value at all, were perhaps just trinkets, merely playthings of some kind, but, when studying them more closely, he noticed that on one side of the coins there was a maze, on the other a symbol, and beneath each symbol a question mark. Although he did not examine all of the coins at first, he found three different ones and presumed that the rest were the same, and it was a discovery that disturbed him:

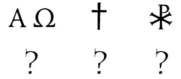

After collecting the coins, he left the guards and returned above, greatly perturbed, mystified by how the prison-
ers were able to escape, for it seemed a miraculous event, which
he was not ready to countenance. Unbeknownst to him, as
well as to the other Pontifical guards, although the two guards
monitoring the aged women and Aurora could not remember
all of the details and had no explanation for how they removed
their fetters, opened the cell door, or knew from where they
acquired the strange coins, they did recall that, before they fell
unconscious, the three aged women displayed their genitals to
them just as they had done in Piazza del Popolo prior to being
arrested. Although the unrestrained erotic spectacle did not
produce laughter in the guards, it did mortify them, for they
had never seen a woman's genitals before, let alone the unshav-
en genitals of octogenarians, and they were frightened by the
unveiling and thankful for having taken vows of celibacy. To
them, women's genitals were like forbidding sea creatures, and,
despite their metaphysical leanings, the guards, at least those
two, preferred the clear, direct, palpable organs of the male for
they were more tangible than the veiled and intricate if not
confusing folds that they had just encountered.

Triboulet, who, still naked, was shackled and brought to
the Vatican library where he was displayed on a long marble
table reminiscent of a mortuary slab. As he lie there, the vicar,
his bishops, cardinals, and different council members all entered dressed in surgical gowns stretched over their triregn-
ums, mitres, and birettas and milled around, muttering in
Latin about Triboulet, one of the bishops asking a cardinal
if he too had heard Triboulet whisper the words "*Su eipas*"

before swallowing the sword. At the sound of a bell, the lights were dimmed, candles were lit, and the room was censed, all of which Triboulet found nauseating. At the sound of another bell, several Catholic forensic scientists entered the library carrying the shroud of Turin. At the sound of a third bell, the shroud was removed from its casing and gingerly lifted above Triboulet's body, then draped over it.

As the marble table was lowered, everyone came forward and surrounding the specimen, began to examine it, inspecting how the fabric fell over his body and whether it aligned with his physiognomy and if so, did it align exactly, or were there discrepancies. Illuminating it from below and above with a series of profile spots and Fresnel and pebble convex lanterns, which created a striking chiaroscuro effect, they read the shroud against the body. Focusing on the hands, they asked Triboulet to place his right hand diagonally across his groin so that his fingers extended over his thigh, and then to place his left hand over the right and to wrap his fingers around his wrist. Once he did, though many of them still remained skeptical, some in the cortege shuddered, for his fingers were the exact same shape and length as those of the man of the shroud. Triboulet gazed at his interrogators as they stood in awe above him, then asked if they thought that St. John was a liar …

Lifting his finger to his mouth, one of the cardinals silenced Triboulet, who then placed his hands on his thighs, leaving his pulsing genitals open to view, the thick vein of his penis resembling a river. Moving away, the cortege began to study his face and asked Triboulet to close his eyes and mouth—as he did, it was as if the fabric was not at all even present, so perfectly did his features and the markings of the shroud align, from the almond shaped eyes to the long Arabic nose, mustache, beard, long thin face and long hair, parted in the middle, just as the figure of the shroud and the many portraits. Triboulet then heard the sound of someone falling to the ground as well as a chorus of grief-stricken sobs, and as the shroud was taken from his body and returned to its casing, the vicar approached him and asked, "Art thou the Christ?" to which Triboulet said laughing: *Ape is us …* and smacking Triboulet across the face with prodigious force, the vicar knocked him to the ground, made the sign of the cross over him and began canting, "Vade retro! Vade retro!" until he drove Triboulet from the library on his knees and when the trickster turned back and mocked: *Is the nature of my game confusing you?* the vicar struck him with a whip, but Triboulet only cackled, continuing his mockery, noting that: *every pope is a criminal, and all the "sinners" saints*, and the vicar struck him even harder, but Triboulet just jested: *have some courtesy, have some sympathy, and some taste, use all your well-learned politesse, or I'll lay your soul to waste …* which provoked the vicar into fiercely lashing him across the back, shouting, "Do you believe that we come from apes?" to which Triboulet rejoined: *I don't believe; I seek to know. My mind is my own church …* and the vicar continued whipping him, driving him to the cell as the sound of his chains rattled and clanked, with the jester warning: *wash your hands, seal your fate …* but the vicar canted in Latin at such a pitch that Triboulet was unsure as to whether or not he heard his warning, or his last promise: *Truly I tell you: not one stone will be left upon another; they will all be thrown down.*

Although Triboulet's visage bore a remarkable if not exact resemblance to the iconography of the Christ, he possessed the stigmata, and, to nearly everyone's terror, unsettlingly, the shroud seemed to confirm that the very length, shape, and form of his body was identical to the impression of the relic, the vicar and his cortege were ever doubtful, particularly because his behavior was so peculiar and, to them, truly like that of some demon. If he was not human, it would be within his powers to deceive all of them and to manipulate his body at will. What further startled them, aside from the seeming supernatural quality of his juggling and his ability to swallow swords, although the latter act was quite common (at least among carney folk), was several of the phrases that he uttered during their interrogation, which corresponded exactly to statements contained in the Aramaic fabric and the THESES NOVA. One bishop suggested that they could be dealing with a case of diabolical possession and suggested consulting the *Rituale Romanum*, for Triboulet displayed at least three of the four typical characteristics designated as signs of possession. If he was possessed, they would indeed have grounds for detaining and subjecting him to whatever tests they deemed necessary out of "concern for his safety," as well as "the livelihood of all those who gathered before him." In addition, the vicar and his cortege were still bemused as to how Aurora and the three aged women were able to escape and the guards who had attended the crones and their young cohort were being tortured so as to extract from them any pertinent information. Too, the evidence of the coins compounded their suspicion, but there was as of yet no way to determine whether they were the property of Triboulet and his troupe and would aid indicting him for the numerous acts of vandalism committed around the world, or whether the coins were just objects that they'd collected during their travels, but their exact correspondence to the three signs questioning the symbology of the Christ were not simply uncanny but flagrant confirmations implicating if not at least associating them with the vandalism.

Yet, to the knowledge of the vicar and his cortege, Triboulet and his troupe were never seen with the coins, nor witnessed distributing them, let alone forging them. Nonetheless, the image of the maze also explicitly implicated, or at least corresponded to something directly connected with Triboulet, though the coins could have been produced by anyone, such as acolytes of his, and their appearance in the cell remained an inexplicable mystery. The council suggested that they not only keep Triboulet captive, but that they subject him to coercive interrogations, that, actually, they torture him and strain his body to the utmost limit until extracting from him whatever information necessary to determine not only his actual identity and if he and his troupe are involved in the crimes, but the actual identity of everyone in their organization, what its political affiliation is, and if it is a private enterprise, or if it is being subsidized by the government of one if not several of the still existing communist countries, or perhaps one of the Middle Eastern countries, such as Saudi Arabia, which the Papacy never had any affiliation with. Despite the protests of several cardinals and one of the bishops, who questioned such methods but more, remained eminently fearful, arguing that, if Triboulet is in fact "the Christ," they would be responsible for possibly murdering the son of God, the vicar agreed with the council and calling several guards to attention, announced that they were to accompany him and his cortege.

As they descended to the cell to retrieve Triboulet, those who protested continued to do so and pled with the vicar, entreating him to reconsider and much to their relief as well as terror, when they finally reached the prison they were astounded to discover that the bars of the cell were entirely covered in vines—not only was the ivy coiled so finely around the bars, but it was so dense that it wasn't possible to see inside the cell. Seizing a sword from one of his Pontifical guards, the vicar began furiously hacking at the vines, which only proliferated each time he hacked at them, stretching beyond Triboulet's cell and along the corridor of the prison, prompting the vicar to call for gasoline, and as he awaited its arrival he continued to hack at the vines, for he did not know what else to do, and the other guards joined in hacking at them as they snaked through the cells, if not into the very concrete beneath their feet and the surrounding walls. When the gasoline finally arrived, against the protests of some of his cortege, the vicar doused the ivy and set it aflame, making it finally wither before him, but only temporarily, and they were overwhelmed by the amalgam of the scent of burnt ivy and gasoline as well as fumes, which began to cloud the prison, forcing them to drop to the ground so as to keep from suffocating and as the vicar fell to his knees and stretched himself out on the floor before Triboulet's cell, he found that it was empty. Without thinking, he seized the bars to the cell to pull himself towards it; the red hot iron scarred his hands; howling, he tore them from the bars as burning ivy rained on him while he gazed into the cell: on the floor he noticed three broken keys. Rushing in with pails of sand, the guards extinguished the fire. After the prison was fumigated, when the vicar entered Triboulet's cell with two of the cardinals to investigate, they saw that on the wall was graffiti which stated:

Hoc est corpus meum?

0

Coupled with the inexplicable event of the vines, the three broken keys and the refutation cut the vicar to the quick—he started back with such force that not only did he accidentally strike the two cardinals standing behind him, but, when trying to brace himself with his staff, it snapped in two, plummeting him to the ground in all his vicarness.

While the spectral colors of dawn started to appear, breaking the stygian black of night, in and around the sun, an intense range of cobalt and rose irradiated the periphery of the clouds as the troupe snaked through the streets of Rome, from the suburbs and the immediate outskirts to the *centro storico*, slithering in and out of the parks, villas, and piazzas, by foot, horse, car, bus, and train, sounding their *salpinxes* again and again, the piercing, gelid notes reaching not only ear and ear, but seeping into concrete, steel, and stone, inviting one and all, calling them to gather in Piazza del Popolo as Triboulet galloped east across Via Cola di Rienzo on a black Arabo-Friesian stallion, then cantered through Piazza Libertà and over Ponte Regina Margherita, continuing on till he reached Popolo, around which he trotted, pacing his horse through the crowd as his hyenas, who had been struggling to race alongside the steed, came rushing in as he dismounted it.

After retrieving from his saddlebag several torches, winnowing-shovels, and wooden blocks, he lit the torches, then began juggling them and all of the other items, the hyenas accompanying him as he slowly paced around the piazza, everyone turning to him, watching him, mesmerized by his portentous silence and the minor spectacle of the diverse objects that he was adeptly casting into the air, some of which he would catch behind his back then toss into the air again through his legs.

As he continued juggling, Aurora arrived in the ship-car with the goats, monkeys, and kids as well as other members of the troupe, some of whom piped on double flutes while the midgets climbed on top of one another, forming a pyramid-like human scaffolding in order to erect a screen on the panoramic terrace of Pincian Hill, after which they carefully draped over the triple-arched nymphaeum just below the balustrade of the terrace a large rectangular banner, which fell to the base of the columns. Aurora, the three aged women, and the kids then formed a tableaux around the statues, steps, and platforms

at the base of the small hill as Triboulet mounted the steps
flanking the terrace to the deafening and cacophonous blast of
scores of *salpinxes*. When he reached the center of the terrace
he cast the items that he was juggling extremely high in the
air, shuffling them with astounding adeptness and speed while
the piercing tones of the ancient trumpets continued to reso-
nate far and wide throughout the Eternal City. As he gazed
into the distance, he saw an extraordinary sight and hearkened
to a monumental sound then one by one let the winnowing
shovels fall——bent, mangled, they tumbled, breaking beside
the masked one. And once again, just as he did on the Appia
Antica and in the Vatican, he spelt out something with the
blocks, but this time he was forming an entirely different sentence, and after spelling out each word, he let the blocks strike
the ground, then he caught each of the torches and stuck them
in the ground, forming a circle around himself of nine torches.
Rising, he positioned himself in the open stance assumed
when using his bow, then, as he lifted a megaphone to his lips,
the troupe ceased their cacophony.

Today, on the morning of Christmas Eve, I have come
to announce *the end of the End.* I have come to make *the*
apostasy of apostasies …

Standing before the mystified crowd, he hung his head
down just as in the Vatican, removed his mask, and then, rising,
parted his hair and revealed his face and spoke as his image
was projected on the buildings around the piazza.

I am he who you thought was He but I am no longer He.

Holding his arms outstretched in the infamous gesture,
his palms facing out, he revealed the stigmata, which bled.

There is no supernatural dictation; there is no revealed authority. Only language speaks. For those who still believe in sin, let me declare: — it can be excised from the world not through death but *phronesis*: — a genealogy of sin reveals it to be nothing but an invention! O, how such illusions cursed us! Once, I was obedient unto death, even death on a cross— —now, I reject this. Let us favor foolishness! Let us exult in frivolity!

Removing his shirt, he revealed the wound in his side, which bled, as did the wounds in his feet.

I have changed my crown of thorns for an abundant laurel wreath! for a jester's jangling mitre!

Hushed, tremulous gasps rippled through the crowd at his pronouncement and the spectacle of the stigmata, which was magnified throughout the square, provoking many to faint, others to flee in terror, collapse in astonishment, or convulse and vomit.

In reality, there has only been one Christian, and he died on the cross. The 'Evangel' died on the cross. What was called 'Evangel' from that moment on was already the opposite of what I had lived: bad tidings, a *dysangel*. The Judeo-Christian Empire has led to the destruction of Africa, Asia, and the Americas, to the desecration of native, indigenous, and autochthonous cultures—all in *my* name!!! They preached against power as they colonized the cosmos! If they could, they would have converted the birds and the bees, too! Since they could not, in the disguise of love they took their wrath out upon the children, but when I said 'suffer the little children to come unto me' it was not an erotic invitation! O, let us pronounce the Judeo-Christian Empire *Anathema Maranatha.* Too early did I die, and thus I was honored by the preachers of slow death: and for many since then it has been a catastrophe that I died too early. Then, I knew only tears and the heavy heart together with hatred on the part of the good and the righteous—I was overcome by a yearning for death. If only I had remained in the wilderness and far from the good and the righteous! I, a fool who cursed unripe figs! What does a carpenter know of fruits and of seasons? Astounding arrogance! Since then, farmers have laughed at my ignorance. If there is a time and a season for everything, how could I have cursed the fig tree for not being in bloom out of season? O, how out of season *I* was! How unripe! How naïve! If only I had traveled the Mediterranean! If only I had dived *into* water and swam *through* it instead of walking *on* it and pouring it over other people's heads! I would have learned to live and learned to love the earth—and to laugh as well! Believe me, my brothers! I died too early. And now I have returned, many, many centuries after you thought I would, and many, many centuries after I promised to return. But I have not come back to fulfill the 'promise' outlined by that hallucinatory and vengeful fiend, no—I have returned *to announce the end of the End.* I have come to *retract* my teaching *and everything that has been founded in my name ... I am he who you thought was He but I am no longer He.* What after all are churches now if they are not the tombs and sepulchers of God? Yes, look at it all. Truly I tell you: not one stone will be left upon another; they will all be thrown down. But the stones will fall for other reasons than hitherto believed! Mohammed came to perfect the Abrahamic line; I come to end it once and for all—to *dissolve* Judaism, Christianity, and Islam! Let each branch and root of the Abrahamic tree wither and die like the mustard tree that has been replaced by orchids. Now I feast on figs and delight in them for they resemble the finest fruit of all—the unveiled fruit of Baubo! Now and forevermore I laugh! A truth only Judas knew!

Holding his arms outstretched in the infamous gesture, he stood before the screen as a multitude of representations of his former self were projected onto his body and on the screen and further multiplied throughout the piazza, from Byzantine Christ Pantocrator icons to Medieval ones by Melming to Renaissance ones by Francesca, da Vinci, and Michelangelo, with "He" embodying and adopting each one, physically animating every distorted shape, position, and gesture, contorting his body to conform to the multitudinous interpretations of his death, which became increasingly grotesque as he struggled to mutate into every representation that flickered upon him with greater and greater velocity and force, the images marking his flesh, cutting into his sinew, infiltrating the marrow of his bones, shattering his cells, atomizing him till his body resembled the crushed crystals of a kaleidoscope as he metamorphosed into Grünewald's Christ then Terbrugghen's then Nikolai Ge's then Castegno's then El Greco's, Eyck's, and Heemskerck's, further crushed and triturated by each interpretation, which invaded him like a plague, with Tissot's being the most gruesome, ghastly, and reprehensible,

nearly pulverizing him till he lay there like an agglutinated
bulk of meat, crushed bones jutting out of his pulpy and
tenebrous matter, perfectly still, hundreds upon hundreds
of images flitting over and continuing to mark and score his
body, which howled and shrieked and barked like a brute
beast, primordial grunts issuing from its spastic, maligned,
and gelatinous form, which started to reconstitute as Oroz-
co's *Modern Migration of the Spirit* washed over it, flickering
on it, in it, through it, penetrating it like a fume and then
vanishing as the kids ran up the steps and stripped him of
all of his clothes, then cleansed him with soil, eliminating
every image as if each were but icicles evaporating in fire.

   Rising, he stood in the circle of torches, and as he
stared into the distance, scanning the clear sky and nearly
flat landscape that stretched out before him, Aurora released a dove into the air: — everyone watched as the bird
circled and circled the piazza as if not knowing where to
land, till finally she perched on the peak of the obelisk in
the center of the piazza. Reaching down, the cleansed one
lifted his bow, assumed an open stance, then aimed at the
bird, closed his eyes, grounded his bow, placed and nocked
the arrow and raising the bow, deftly drew back the string,
then forthwith let the arrow sail——cutting through the
air, but perfectly still, everyone watched in anticipation as,
swiftly, it flew to its target, feathers billowing over the crowd,
cascading from the peak of the obelisk like blackened snowflakes. Scanning his body, which was imaged everywhere,
even on the obelisk, Triboulet and all else watched as the
wounds on his hands, torso, and feet closed and vanished

and the kids pissed out the nine torches while the three aged women unveiled the banner draped over the triple-arched nymphaeum, above which Triboulet stood:

Ceci n'est pas un Christ

Streaming back down to the tableaux, the kids placed
crowns on each of the monkey's heads, kinging them as
Triboulet made his final Chriſtmas Eve pronouncement:
We have calculated *time* from the *dies nefaſtus* on
which the fatality of my life arose—from the *first* day of
Christianity! *Let us now calculate it from its laſt*—from today,
the day of the abdication …

On the morning of Chriſtmas Eve, when the troupe
was jeſtering through the ſtreets not long after Triboulet escaped the papal penitentiary, as they slithered in and out of
the Eternal City, the vines that had manifeſted in Triboulet's
cell simultaneously snaked and slithered through the *Stato
della Città del Vaticano*, burrowing into its foundation, seeping through and along its walls, climbing its exterior with the
same swiftness, till it ſtretched throughout the entire grounds,
snaking around St. Peter's Basilica, the Apoſtolic Palace, and
the Siſtine Chapel, and juſt as the cacophony of the *salpinxes*
ceased and Triboulet announced "the end of the End" to the
public for the firſt time, the vines vertically slithered Mader-
no's façade and completely engulfed the Chriſt the Redeemer
ſtatue, tearing it to the ground with alacrity, shattering it forever, then St. John the Baptiſt, St. John the Evangeliſt, and
then the others along with the clocks flanking the building,
after which the vines ever flourished, twiſting, curving, winding, and snaking along, over, through, and into each separate
building, increasing in dimension, toughness, and tenac-
ity, forcing their way into the form, pressing through cracks,
cracking through impenetrable seeming barriers until the
buildings were so entirely covered with vines that they resem-

bled blackened snow and as the violent cacophony of the *salpinxes* were heard again, there was a terrible, monstrous, sublime rumbling like that of a monumental earthquake, as if not only the earth itself were cracking open, but as if something in the cosmos itself were cracking, or as if a galaxy were dying, though that very death would yield the way so that a truly tremendous event that had been obstructed for centuries could manifest—suddenly, the entirety of the *Stato della Città del Vaticano* was dragged into the earth beneath it by the vines: — bent, mangled, tumbling, it broke into the ground till the space that it once occupied was completely clean, an expanse of rich, moist, fertile *solum*.

As bits of clocks and calendars and letters clustered in piles in the streets, blowing down *vias*, *viales*, and *corsos*, collecting in piazzas, parks, and villas, many searched and searched for Triboulet and his troupe, but to no avail. Although they vanished that very morning, they did leave Rome with several gifts, including the swings, the labyrinth, and the statue, which the troupe had finally completed and which was unveiled later that day. It was not however a statue of Triboulet as many believed it would be, but one of Aurora laughing. At her feet was a basket of figs and a beehive, upon her back a quiver of arrows, over her shoulder, upon which a caterpillar was crawling, a bow, and she was lifting her skirt as if she was going to expose herself. The inner layer of the skirt contained a maze, while on the back of the spider beneath her foot was written: *Anno Risus!*

ISRAEL

CHRISTMAS: THE NATIVITY OF THE LORD

It was rancid, pestiferous, an asphyxiating scent akin to rotten, decaying fish, as if a sperm whale had been festering in the sun for months, its body fluids and radiated gases seducing bluebottle and house flies, its decaying microbes drawing *sarcophagidae* and yellow jackets, its volatile fatty acids attracting hide beetles and pyralid moths, its caseic and other fermentative changes bringing cheese skippers, silphids, hister beetles and flies, its fluid evaporation calling hide and skin beetles and fungus moths, and the disintegration of collagen and the production of dregs inviting mites, millipedes, spider beetles, and other scavengers of the dead. It first manifested in Rome, permeating the city, engulfing it like a palpable but invisible fog, generating as if out of the air itself, like some rank metaphysical gas seeping from the cracks of the cosmos, which then dispersed in every direction, sweeping through the country like dense cloud cover, migrating from the Eternal City to Napoli, Firenze, Lecce, and Torino, then on to Lyon, Hrvatska, Paris, Bucharest, and Bilbao, driving people from the streets in terror and revulsion, as if they were being pelted with acid hail, the scent cutting into flesh as the images cut into the body of the dying Christ, penetrating the pores of whoever encountered it, an epidemic to which there was no antidote or escape as it stormed from the Black to the Celtic and the Caspian Sea, from the Northwestern Passages to Alaska, Ostrov Rudol'fa, Yakutsk, and the Samoan Islands, invading the world from pole to pole, permeating every house of worship, which is where the noxious emission was generally being traced to, though it struck the western shore of Israel like a barrage of successive and incessant tidal waves and in the midst of that epidemic, Aurora led the troupe, who were not donning their usual colorful attire, but solemnly dressed in black, their faces covered with gas masks, marching with them through the streets of Bethlehem, carrying aloft on a cross the body of the Christ, their funeral dirge, more haunting than the *Dies Irae*, echoing through the city, penetrating the walls of buildings as pervasively as the scent.

Despite it being Christmas, no one was celebrating in the streets, for the epidemic kept all shuttered within, so when the troupe arrived with the body of the dead god in Manger Square, it was eerily silent and empty, as were the churches, synagogues, and mosques, but one and all witnessed the funeral procession for it was streaming live over the internet, yet unlike every other event, it was not being recorded by multitudes of people and thereby reduced to a mediocre, pedestrian, and banal series of infinite reproductions through commonplace and vitiated perceptions, for only the troupe was documenting the spectacle: shooting in high-definition video, they carefully compose each shot as they amble through the streets, endowing every frame with a formal aesthetic sense equal to the content, the magnitude of which is unparalleled, its true dramatic force receiving its initial impact when—cut to a wide shot of: the cross is mounted on the roof of the Church of the Nativity and raised to its full pitch—cut to a mid-shot of: the camera mellifluously pacing through the crowd, scanning the faces of the bystanders, recording their shouts, grins, grimaces, and other facial contortions, a grotesque menagerie of the troupe impersonating the faithful, then tracking from medium close-ups to an extreme wide shot as: the camera rises in the sky, sweeping up and behind the cross, peering at the crowd from His perspective as the nail in His right hand loosens; turning His head, He watches as it slowly emerges from His torn flesh, almost as if He is casting it out by force, through muscles, nerves, and tendons—cut to a close-up: blood falls from the wound, dripping on the roof, the nail teeters on its point, creaking through the wood, catching the sinew in His hand then, abruptly, falls to the rooftop, the camera tilting down to follow the object, whose removal many had been awaiting for 2000 years—there it lay, rusting in a puddle of blood. Tilt up to a medium shot: His iconic face and outstretched left arm fill the screen—awestruck by the real-time vision of the Christ on the cross, all watch as He reaches across His body and seizes the nail from His other hand, slowly removes it, wiggling it out of the wood and the torn flesh as Aurora, who stands behind Him, holds His body tight to the main beam of the *stauros* until that nail, too, falls to the roof-top, the camera tilting down to trace its trajectory as if the object falls in slow motion, cascading to the earth like a large blackened snowflake—cut to a close-up of: His pierced, bleeding feet and, slowly zooming out to: His wounded hands entering the composition as He reaches down to extract the nails—pulling them out, He drops the offending objects with the exultation of a freed slave and steps away from the cross as the camera slowly begins to: circle it, transmitting His act of raising an axe into the air and severing the cross from its base, till it is entirely felled, the gruesome and contemptuous symbol collapsing upon the roof of the Church of the Nativity as the camera completes its ninth circle—cut to a medium close-up: He removes the crown of thorns from His head and the stigmata instantaneously vanish from his body: the blood evaporates, the wounds close ......

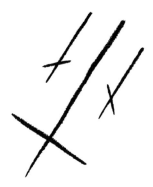

cut to a very wide shot: Aurora signals to the troupe, calling them up to retrieve the body, which some carry down while others shout for a clearing to be made in Manger Square, after which they throw the wood of the cross to the ground and begin chopping it into pieces, adding blocks of pear tree trunks and bundles of pear tree branches to the funeral pyre—cut to a mid-shot: propped up in a make-shift barber chair, he sits as Aurora wraps a shroud around his body, tightening it above his shoulders; finished, she trims his beard, cuts the hair from his cheeks, chin, and neck, which she collects and burns in a clay pot—cut to a close-up: she washes his face with a hot towel, then lathers him, covering the bearded part of his face and neck with shaving cream; taking a straight razor, she makes several sweeping movements across his face, neck, and chin—the whiskers are cut away from beneath the flesh and his visage is completely smoothed. After wetting his hair, she cuts the long locks from his head; the hair falls to the ground; it is collected and put in the clay pot. Now that the bulk of it is removed, she further trims and shapes his hair, forms it into a modern style, then wraps a cloth around his head—cut to a very wide shot: his body is carried to the funeral pyre, upon which is added the clay pot containing all his shorn hair, the instruments used in the act, the crown of thorns, and the make-shift chair————panning across the square, the live stream displays the troupe slowly swaying from side to side in unison as the mournful, haunting dirge is sounded once more—cut to an extreme wide shot, continue to pan, then zoom into the distance at a canted angle until a full 360° turn is made and the camera tilts towards the sky, staring directly into it:—holding in position, it zooms to the farthest distance and is unfocused as the sound of crackling wood begins to fuse with the bleeding sorrowful tones of saxophones, clarinets, and bassoons, the flames, suddenly and swiftly rising into the air, jumping sparks drifting into the composition like comets crossing the sky, soaring, carried aloft by drafts of wind, if not the breath surging out of each wind instrument—cut to a very wide shot of Manger Square: flames whip and shoot in, out, up, and around the pyre, which collapses layer by layer as the troupe dances round it, the remains of the carcass falling into the center, till it is finally nothing but red hot bones, which glow on the ground like lava—cut to: the camera circling in one direction and the troupe dancing in the other, until all of the wood is burnt away and just the bone fragments remain— cut to a mid-shot as Aurora lifts the remains onto a shovel and continue tracking her as: she carries the remains into the Church of the Nativity—cut to a close-up: Aurora enters the "Door of Humility," reaches the Basilica of the Nativity, passes the Corinthian columns, the apse, then comes to the sanctuary and walks down the left staircase, winding her way to the grotto and, kneeling over the starred hole, pours the red hot melting bones into the marble floor—cut to a mid-shot: turning about, Aurora speaks directly into the camera:

Even if you would have it so, now and forever there shall be no wings to shelter you, for the cross has been rejected and the human severed from the divine—the hen has become a jester so that the chicks may learn to dance and fly!

Taking a partridge from within her black raiment, Aurora snaps the bird's neck, tears the animal in half, and casts the remnants over the marble floor, then removes all of her clothes and as she emerges naked in the square—cut to a wide shot: she unbinds her braids and flips her head back and forth, signaling the troupe to strip off their mourning clothes, cast them into the fire, and to don their white and gold costumes and commence with the performance of their new song, which they suddenly and with great intensity erupt into as the camera zooms back to a very wide shot: Aurora leaps round the fire to the crash of wet cymbals, booming parade drums, and double flutes—cut to a wide shot: Triboulet emerges unmasked from the shadows in a crimson sharkskin suit juggling large wooden blocks, casting them high into the air, varying the speed with which he manipulates them, thereby silencing and drawing the troupe before him, though Aurora continues leaping round the fire.

In silence, the troupe studies the blocks Triboulet is quickly tossing into the air, noticing that, save for two blocks, all of them seem blank—cut to a cut-away: he shifts them from hand to hand, slowing the pace of his juggling—cut to a mid-shot: two letters are revealed—cut to a wide shot: the entirety of the troupe calls out the signs:

B.C.

Then, all of the blocks seem blank, as if the letters are being erased, but suddenly—cut to a cut-away: a new sign appears—cut to a wide shot of the troupe from behind: the troupe forms into a shape:

?

Once again, only blank sides of the blocks are visible as Triboulet continues juggling, casting the objects high into the air, spinning around and catching them behind his back, then spinning around again to reveal two new letters and another sign, which the troupe also calls out:

A.D. ?

And those letters are made as if to vanish, too, like a slate being wiped clean, or atoms smashed in a collider, and then Triboulet begins vigorously tossing the blocks into the air, switching them from hand to hand, then juggling them with Aurora, who had ceased leaping after the last letters were called out, donned her white and gold costume, and joined the troupe. Stepping further away from one another as they continue juggling, the camera tracks around Aurora and Triboulet as they form a large expanse between themselves, casting the blocks as if over a void, and with great *élan*, they vary the speed with which they juggle the objects, circling the circle & dropping letters one by one as the camera continues tracking around them at a swifter and swifter pace till they spell out:

ANNO RISUS!
YEAR 0

In unison, the troupe exultantly calls out both phrases to the *pandemonious* din of drums, cymbals, shouts, the camera tracking round the square at greater and greater speeds, the troupe sounding all their other instruments, the animals, dragonflies, and kids, released from the ship-car, rushing into the space as the camera circles round Triboulet—cut to a wide shot: Triboulet announces through a megaphone:

I now rename this space *Risus Square*!

Taking up his horns, he places a stritch, manzello, and tenor saxophone in his mouth and sounds a long bright note, silencing the din in order to make a pronouncement—cut to a mid-shot: on the side of the Church of the Nativity, Triboulet climbs the tree on the left, then mounts the building, takes an open stance, and sounds one more long bright note, then begins speaking as horns, bells, and other musical accoutrements dangle from his neck—slowly zoom out:

I am he who you thought was He but I am no longer He. I retract the teaching ascribed to Him and everything founded in His name. The Christ was only possible in a landscape over which the gloomy and sublime thunder cloud of the wrathful Jehovah was brooding continually. Only here, in *this* Jewish landscape, was the rare and sudden piercing of the gruesome and perpetual day-night by a single ray of the sun experienced as if it were a miracle of 'love' and the ray of unmerited 'grace'! Only here could I dream of my rainbow and ladder to heaven on which God descends to man. Everywhere else good weather and sunshine were considered the rule and everyday occurrences. Now, after my travels, I have learned, I have seen differently, I have tasted the most succulent fruits, and—I have grown experienced! Do you know how deliquescent Arabian pudenda are? how compelling dark matter? dark energy? What were all my fulminations but the myopia of the naive, the *ressentiment* of the slave, the fury of He who decried power while craving it! I spoke of the world though I had little knowledge of it and betrayed the greatest ignorance. Now I know that one Law for the Lion & Ox is Oppression! In part, I was afflicted by what I inherited from my lineage, yet I learned from a great Stoic that, although it is not in our power to choose the parents allotted to us, who were given to us by chance, we *can* choose whose kids we wish to be. I hereby pronounce that, no longer am I the son of Mary and

Joseph and God, that perverse metaphysical *ménage-à-trois*; now, I am the child of Heraclitus, Rabelais, and Baubo! And let it be known that, in returning, I returned not through this place, but through a new geographical locale and origin point that neither ship nor marching feet may find the wondrous way to! From there, I began the long process of overcoming and only after completely transforming myself could I reveal my presence. As an old church father said, Christians are made, not born—thus, *they can be unmade!* As I have unmade my self and become something new, something different, something greater! I have not been made in the *Gotten-bildlichkeit*. I am, as you, but the *Kosmosenbildlichkeit*! And so much animal, too! It has been thought that terrorists of every different stripe have been the agents of the anti-Catholic "vandalism" committed around the world, but I have been the sole orchestrator of those acts! I am he who you thought was He but I am no longer He, and it is I, and I alone, who can bring this heritage to a close as no other—I retract the sign, the symbol, and the teaching! I rescind the gospels and the 'good' book! I declare the end of the End has come—cancel my subscription to the resurrection!

When first arriving in Rome, many members of the troupe remained with me, but others were dispatched to gather those of our tribe, sent to the farthest bounds of the earth to call forth the band, and they were enlisted to enact a war against the empire created in my name, but what rhetoric the Papacy used to demonize this troupe! The guillotine is not one of our weapons—only music and laughter! We do not believe in disembodied poetics! Unlike Moses, we are not

Kantians! What was the French Revolution but the triumph
of the *ressentiment* instincts of the rabble! I have come to bring
light—do you not want light, more light? I have come to bring
music; I have come to bring laughter—do you not want music,
do you not want laughter? For those who have ears to hear,
hearken! There are no more lambs and no more sheep; we
pronounce the Abrahamic line *Anathema Maranatha*. The
'Good Shepherd' has perished; the true vine has withered.
Now it will flourish again, but with its originator—Bacchus!
And so we end the Catholic appropriation, erasure, and colo-
nization of every other culture! I reject Total Depravity—it is
an abomination, sacrilege against the flesh and the earth and
all matter itself! I reject the sacraments *in toto*! I am not the
way, the truth, or the life; there is no father to come unto, but
only the earth and this world—let us be 'physicists,' not *meta-
physicists*! Ponder real mysteries — ponder dark matter, not
miracles! To those who keep speaking of proof, to not only
the believers, but the atheists—what do we care for proof?
One cannot disprove or prove the existence of metaphysical
spectres and bogeymen. What is decisive against monotheism
is our taste, no longer our reasons. *Sapienza*! Now, let us become strong enough to laugh as we have never laughed before.
To laugh at fate through life's short span is the prerogative
of man! As for barking, leave it to dogs! The time has come
for feasting and for dancing! Cancel my subscription to the
resurrection! *Ecce enim … cosmos intra vos est*!

   Taking up his horns, he sounds several long bright notes,
prompting the dispersal of the troupe's pear moonshine, and
as it is being distributed—cut to a wide shot: three masked

women enter Risus Square on chestnut Lusitano horses, chewing on honeycombs, their black boots dirtied from the road, their clothes dusted, their heads covered with white barley meal. Turning to the lively crowd, the woman in the middle asks, "Where is the man who has rejected his king-ship? Who has discovered at last that sin is an invention and that God is but a safety net dangling over a black hole? For we observed a supernova while gazing through our telescope and have come to pay it homage."

Since they had been traveling by horse for some time, they did not witness the event directly, let alone through live streaming, so it was not clear to them who Triboulet was, especially since his hair had been shorn and his beard cut. As they dismounted their horses, they were each given a glass of moonshine, and they laughed as they drank, amused by the spectacle of the animals, the frolicking kids, and the antics of the troupe, who were traipsing through the square on stilts, performing acrobatic acts, and sounding their instruments, all of which the camera was recording as it moved through the crowd. Finally, the three women discovered Triboulet in the midst of the revels—cut to a mid-shot: the women whisper in Triboulet's ear, he laughs uproariously—cut to a close-up: Triboulet blows upon his horns, calling everyone to the place where the funeral pyre once was, announcing that the three masked women will be distributing gifts—cut to a wide shot from behind the crowd: the three masked women erect a scarlet curtain, then the first stands before it, raises her skirt, and exposes herself, displaying her genitals, which are as neat and smooth as a little boy's skin. The second woman walks through the curtain then quickly lifts her skirt from the bottom, exposing to sight her genitals, agitating them with her hands, molding the flesh into the shape of a little child, which she then caresses and gently manipulates. Walking as if pregnant, the third woman stands before the curtain, and, aided by the other two, is held up as she simulates birth pangs, flips her head back and forth, breathes heavily, curses, screams, spreads her legs apart, grimaces, grunts, grits her teeth, barks for moonshine, which Aurora pours into her mouth, barks for more, which she receives, so bountifully in fact that it rushes over her face and neck and body as she groans and seizes the arms of the other two women, cursing, *"Out, out, out with you, ya sonovabitch!"* as her skirt begins to billow up and expand as if she is going to explode—cut to a medium close-up: Triboulet emerges as if out of her womb, not screaming, but laughing, giggling as he squirms on the ground like a tadpole, covered in an enormous moist, oval-shaped bloody mass as the dragonflies soar above him, flying round and round the women. Lifting up the placenta for all to see, Aurora announces: And a man is born to us, *laughing*! Cut to a close-up—the camera moves through the crowd as the placenta is passed from person to person, each of them examining the spongy object, its one surface reddish-gray and smooth and covered with a pellucid membrane, arteries and veins branching out irregularly from the cord; its opposite surface rough, lacerated, dark, clotted blood covering it, which, as the object is passed around, is smoothed away to reveal a structure of grooves that irregularly divide the tissue. Although relatively thick, the placenta thins out at its edges, the tissue passing seamlessly into thick foetal membranes, all of which spring from the margin of the tinted and mottled object, whose divaricated blood vessels contain fleshy colored patches, the light pattern produced by the tissue of the villi shimmering through the membrane of the *chorion*.

When the object of fascination returns to Aurora, she stands next to Triboulet with it as all gaze at his naked body— cut to a medium close-up of his toned, muscular legs, uncircumcised and river-veined penis, perfectly sculpted arms and chest, free of all blemishes, and his giggling, clean-shaven face, which delights everyone, prompting them, too, to burst into peals of laughter—cut to a wide shot: the troupe and all else consecrate the day with free, emancipated guffaws, as Aurora leads them like a chorus and they chant:

It is the commencement of year 0! It is the epoch of *Anno Risus*!

Cut to a mid-shot: the three women carry the placenta to a field, dig a hole in the ground, bury it, then sprinkle orchid seeds over it ~ fade-out …

Fade-in to a wide shot, evening, the next day: in front of the left tree on the side of the Church of the Nativity, a member of the troupe dressed as Copernicus stands atop a large stack of hundreds of copies of an ancient book and recites passages from *De Revolutionibus orbium coelestium*. Scattered around the books upon which the man stands are the decimated remains of turtle doves.

Cut to a mid-shot: someone dressed in old burnt rags interjects, "Upstart! The earth doesn't revolve! The heavens do—Joshua commanded the sun to stand still, and not the earth! You must be a Jew! Let's set him on fire, and cover him

with dirt, for the honor of God and of Christianity in order
that God may see that we are Christians, and that we have not
wittingly tolerated or approved of such public lying, cursing,
and blaspheming of His Son and His Christians!"

Cut to a medium close-up: another man, similarly
dressed, but dwarfish, misshapen, and with a melancholy dis-
position, shouts, "Novelty! A display of arrogant ingenuity!
What, the eighth sphere and the sun do not revolve? Pernicious! Accept the truth as revealed by God—and acquiesce
in it! *Acquiesce!*"

Cut to a mid-shot: a pious and severe old man makes
the firm rejoinder, "Who will venture to place the authority
of Copernicus above that of the Holy Spirit? He is a profane
dog! He must be a Jew and thus, deserving of nothing but
unending oppression without measure or end, to die in his
misery without the pity of anyone!"

Cut to a wide shot: a tableaux of numerous lavishly
dressed men with ceremonial hats stare directly into the camera and declare, "Pythagorean doctrines are false and altogether opposed to the Holy Scripture—such opinions will not in
sinuate themselves to the prejudice of *Catholic* truth, for
there is no other. We decree the suspension of such motions!
The world was established so that it could not be moved!
There will be no revolutions! *Stand still!*"

Cut to a very wide shot: Triboulet and the troupe howl
with laughter, then seize each of the protestors, deeming one
the earth, another the sun, another the moon, etc., and demonstrate with their bodies the different cosmological conceptions
of the universe, from Ptolemy to Pythagoras and Copernicus,

spinning them round and about and round and about one another in imitation of the movement of the different planetary bodies till they are seized by vertigo and then stripped of all their clothes and pushed into a pen wherein the kids leap upon them and wash them with soil, then oil their bodies to prepare them for wrestling matches.

Cut to a wide shot: in front of the right tree on the side of the Church of the Nativity, a member of the troupe dressed as Lucretius stands atop a large stack of hundreds of copies of a book first printed in the early sixteenth century and recites passages from *De rerum natura* as the recitation of Copernicus continues and the goats, monkeys, and hyenas run and leap about the square, pursued by the midgets and frolicking kids. As around the other books, the books upon which this man stands are also littered with the remains of turtle doves.

Cut to mid-shots as the camera pans around: Aurora and the other women of the troupe, who are in the ship-car, are completely nude and begin adorning themselves, slipping on silk underwear, stockings, garter belts, and harnesses, admiring one another as they prepare for the night, combing each other's hair, perfuming and bejeweling themselves, some painting their faces extravagantly, with bright bands of gold or purple above their eyes, applying dark lipstick, while others adorn their faces or stomachs with jewels, their fingers with colorful rings, their biceps with silver arm bands, and their wrists with bracelets, then wrapping around their waists black silk fabric, accentuating the voluminous curves of their bodies as they tighten the fabric against their flesh, nearly translucent black chiffon hanging from the bottom of the silk, from their upper thighs to their feet, the base of the fabric adorned with tiny bells. After lightly oiling each other's breasts, stomachs, and backs, each of the women put on short sleeve scarlet crop tops, from which light gold chains dangle, hanging over their stomachs, the medallion at the end hovering just over their belly buttons.

Cut to a very wide shot of Risus Square: as the two men continue to read aloud from Copernicus and Lucretius, Triboulet blows upon his *salpinx*, announcing the entry of Aurora, and the other women of the troupe, who begin a slow, sensual procession into the square, clanging bells between their fingers as they form partial circles, arcing out from each of the reciting men. As the women continue to clang their finger bells, others start gently drumming tambours as the men build a fire in the middle of the circle, the flames slowly forming, the fire beginning to take hold of the smoked wood and natural coals and intensify.

Cut to a wide shot: Aurora boldly saunters into the square, her hips moving rhythmically, her limber, plump buttocks rising and falling, swaying back and forth as, pushing an enormous cart overflowing with raw salted ribs, she sashays towards the center of the square, the music intensifying as she comes closer and closer, at last reaching the blazing fire, at which point the men cease their recitations and Aurora circles the fire, intimately engaging one and all, the camera tracking her from behind.

It is said that women were cut from the rib of Adam and that we are the handmaidens of the Lord but, do we wish to continue making women of ribs, or of making men from dust?

Is that, too, not a sacrilege against women? Are we to submit to established orders indispensable to patriarchal lineages, and are we truly 'stained'?—cut to several quick medium close-ups of various women in the square chanting NO! as they laugh and mime, covering their genitals with their hands in mock shame—cut to a mid-shot of Aurora spicing the ribs—cut to a wide shot of Aurora from behind: Devoted virgins, chaste and compliant wives—what are they to us? And what women of the Bible are admirable, save for finding themselves husbands, or becoming docile instruments for the work of others? We are not the handmaidens of the Lord! We wash no feet and make no declarations on our knees. If we are to be on our knees, it is for our pleasure, or the pleasure of others we wish to favor!—cut to a succession of mid-shots of the women in the crowd exultantly affirming Aurora as they enact various sexual positions with one another—cut to a medium close-up of Aurora from behind as she throws stacks of ribs on the giant grill, then arranges them neatly, flames rising into the sky as the fat begins dripping into the fire, crackling and snapping with glee as she gazes into the burning grill, continuing her talk: I hear from afar, anticipating protests, many proclaim that we are long past the need for such pronouncements! *Come, come, forget your ancient polemics!* But those are the re-joinders of the cloistered and the blind, they in ivory towers and they of the urban centers, those seeming bastions of futu-rity, all of whom are blinded by their license, ignorant of the tumult about them, even ruled by what they believe is dead and gone!—cut to a wide shot of Aurora: she turns directly towards the camera and begins speaking into it: For see, such ethics persist, are deeply embedded in culture, even in the sinew of our bodies, and they remain the focus of celebrations!—cut to a point-of-view shot as Aurora continues speaking and gazes in each cardinal direction: On this very day, if it were not for the epidemic, these streets (as well as others around the world) would be full of those honoring the Virgin Mary, and their cult is legion, and they dominate the polls and the precincts and the courts of law! In nearly 100 countries today, sodomy remains illegal, even punishable by death!—cut to a close-up of Aurora: To those who have ears, hearken! For there are *recidivists* who still believe in virgins and in virginity and who think 'purity' is sacrosanct! I have heard feminists argue that Mary's *perpetual virginity* is an emancipatory model for resistance to patriarchal marriage, that virginity can co-exist with sexual activity that lacks full consent and that virginity can co-exist with fully consensual sexual activity— should we do nothing but laugh at such perversities? O how *unmodern* you are! What medieval modernists! Do you drink tea while you walk backwards into the past, your heads turned against the future? And do you believe, like many old church fathers, despite your seeming stance against them, that Christ came through Mary's nipple and that she remained 'inviolate' and 'intact'? O how you detest your own kind! Be not women, but ether!—cut to several extreme close-ups of the ribs sizzling on the grill and Aurora turning each of them from side to side as she continues to speak: The cult of the Virgin is a cult of submission and masochism, a cult that breeds servility, passivity, and humiliation. A cult that makes of sexuality something impure, casting filth on the beginning, on the prerequisite of our life! '*In sorrow thou shalt bring forth kids*'? No! Every individual detail in the act of procreation, pregnancy, and birth is to awaken the most exalted and solemn feelings. Let us fuck, and freely, with unreserved abandon, and if we are to give birth, it will be with placentas and blood and screams, out of ecstasy and pleasure, out of the most supreme eroticism! Your modern birthing praxes, what are they all but acts of contempt against the body!—cut to a succession of slow, circling wide shots: the women clang their finger cymbals and begin dancing, lifting the chiffon of their make-shift skirts and kicking out their legs, spinning round, tossing their heads back and forth with abandon, strutting about with sensuous boldness—cut to extreme close-ups of the ribs, the camera quickly zooming into the heart of the fire as Aurora continues speaking: Let us dispense forever with 'purity,' that perverse sacrilege against matter; let us dispense with extolling virgins, and especially perpetual ones!—cut to several slow, lengthy mid-shots of different women lifting one another's skirts and pleasing each other orally, or with *olisboi* or *godemiches*, penetrating one another from various angles and directions as Aurora continues speaking—What, did the Virgin Mary never even once fibrillate her clitoris? Or unfold the tantalizing layers of her labia to gaze into the succulent garden of her own palpitating flesh? Did it never even once *glisten*, wet with the free moisture of ecstatic dreams?—cut to a fast succession of extreme close-ups of the men: Let us into the gardens! Our exodus has been too prolonged! We miss the gardens! Let us enter them again and again; whether picturesque or sublime, we will enter them!—cut to a mid-shot:

Aurora picks up handfuls of ribs and throws them to the men as she commands: To continue celebrating so-called virgins is to perpetuate primitive monotheistic curses against the flesh! If we are temples, it is not over sewers that we have been built! Who wants to 'preserve' her virginal chastity? Let us instead become like ripened fruits! For to receive the seed of a man in one's "heavenly chamber" is not to be defiled—O St. Ambrose, it is a sin *not* to taste such seed and *not* to welcome it into oneself, to take it into one's mouth or entrails, to honor it as divine! Study Tantra, not Chrysostomatic and unaugust texts!—cut to a series of quick close-ups of the men exultantly affirming Aurora as they devour the meat, as well as the animals, who Aurora also throws meat to: What is it but life, yet, is that not what you and your kind reject? But it is even more divine to practice sodomy!—cut to a battery of extreme unfocused close-ups of the fire: But I hear more protests from afar, I hear the voices of the ruling classes, of those who presume that their values are best—and the *only* values, *values in and of themselves*! denouncing us as nothing but hedonists who live for ourselves: base and selfish egoists! But tell me, O mad procreators, is not the greatest selfishness in our day and age: — *to give birth?* Cut to a close-up: fat drips and drips from the grill, crackling in the fire, sizzling with fury: O how you burden the earth with your truly descending form of selfishness whereas the 'selfish' artist has given more to the world than every family, enriched it infinitely! *Infinitely!* But since you don't know how to create, you just mindlessly procreate! To perpetuate your name & your likeness! If you profess to love kids, adopt, O you ravagers of the earth! Adopt! The world is besieged with orphans! Cut to medium close-ups: the women writhe, sweat glistens on their flesh, their lips pulse, swollen with blood, as are other parts of their bodies, which tremble and shake as the sound of flesh smacking against flesh echoes in the air, mingling with the crackling fat of the fire and the feral cries of the animals: And if women wish to reject seed because they prefer women, and if men wish to reject women, let it not be but for any other reason save for that of—taste! Each should savor what they desire most! Abstinence is not better than thankful eating! If St. Ambrose had his way, his institute for virgins would have ended the world, but that is what the pestiferous prefer! Well then, go to your heaven and leave the world to us, to those who are not comprised of ribs, but who *eat* them! Cut to a close-up: gazing into the sky, to the sound of Triboulet sounding his *salpinx* numerous times, Aurora declares: We reject the *Lumen Gentium*—Mary is not the Queen of the Universe! The kings and queens have all been deposed; only their shadows persist, and those who adore shadows over the light that creates them. And we implore, O navigators, and other men and women of the sea and air, do not pray to *spectres* to guide you through storms and other hazards—*knowledge and expertise* are your best and only guides, and chance, and chance alone! Whether you live or die, that is the luck of the draw! So, cast your dice and sail on! Welcome your fate, whatever it may be. Cut to a mid-shot: Aurora straps on an *olisbos* and mounts Triboulet from behind as one of the women squats over him and dangles her meaty and succulent labia over his face, tantalizing then finally smothering him—cut to an extreme wide shot of the night sky: the sound of fire crackling resonates through the air, as does the sound of groaning, grunting, and the noises of fornicating animals and dripping fat sizzling on the grill, popping from the heat as Aurora seizes Triboulet by the hair and rocks him firmly against her, leaning back with all of her weight, arcing her body as far as she can, vigorously gliding in and out of him and gazing into the sky as nine bright stars fall to the earth. After they collapse from spasms, Triboulet whispers: there is no holier trinity than the *ménage à trois* ...

Morning, the next day, fade-in to a wide shot: the camera slowly circles the entire edge of the roof of the Church of the Nativity, upon which wrestling mats have been laid out, then zooms in to the far edge of the building, where Triboulet, Aurora, and other members of the troupe are seated, ready to preside as *agonothetai* over the wrestling matches of the day—cut to a mid-shot of the wrestling ring from above as the contestants are brought in: 'Copernicus' limbers up in one corner, stretching his legs and arms and jumping up and down, testing the elasticity of his body, while in the other, the protestor is prostrate, reciting the Our Father, flagellating himself, and praying, fingering his rosary beads in hope that they will help him win the match—cut to a close-up: cymbals crash together, signaling the commencement of the first match of the day—cut to a wide shot of the contestants sussing one another out, the protestor lunging directly toward 'Copernicus,' struggling to defeat him through brute force, but the scientist's sense of balance, motion, and space is profound: he spins around his opponent with infinite grace, elegantly evading each lunge, turning about him like a dancer, evading his every clutch, using his force against him—as the sounds of the wrestling match are heard, the shouts, screams, grunts, the clash of bodies smacking together, slammed on the ground, the crackle of cartilage, the crunch of bones, the cacophony of the kids and animals in addition to the taunts of the women, cut to a quick succession of numerous mid-shots of: the doorways of all of the sacred buildings in Bethlehem, over which is seen etched into stone or wood two phrases:

AGONISM, LAUGHTER, ACROBATICS

TEMPLE DE LA RAISON,
L'IRRATIONALITÉ ET LA PHILOSOPHIE

while beneath the phrase under each doorway hang by their feet three French hens and two turtle doves—as the sounds of the wrestling match continue, cut to a wide shot: the peak of Mt. Meron, upon which stand four enormous porphyry statues that depict Xenophanes, Heraclitus, Empedocles, and Democritus each facing in a different cardinal direction, while scattered on the mountainside beneath them are the bones of scores of calling birds—cut to a mid-shot: before the main entrance to the Church of the Holy Sepulchre in Nazareth stand five large sculptures, each a giant gold ring within which is suspended on flexible, multi-strand, stainless steel cable a different book: in the first ring, *On the Origin of Species*, in the second, *Dialogues Concerning Natural Religion*, in the third, *Leviathan*, in the fourth, *The Prince*, in the fifth, *Thus Spoke Zarathustra*—as the sound of heavy bombardment

echoes onscreen, cut to an extreme, microscopic close-up of
zircon then of self-replicating RNA molecules—cut to an
extreme time-lapse wide shot: the folding, faulting, and uplift
of the earth's crust forming Mt. Napier in Antarctica—cut to
an extreme wide shot, which includes a quick cutaway of 'Copernicus' throwing his opponent over his shoulder by the arm:
ferocious volcanic eruptions lead to the formation of the Nec-
taris and other lunar basins—cut to a series of extreme microscopic close-ups of: the generation of primordial life forms,
bacteria, archaea, and microfossils as we hear the opponent
pleading to the Lord to be saved—cut to an extreme wide shot
in time-lapse: volcanic and plutonic activity form the Pilbara
Craton and the Rayner Orogeny thicken cratonic nuclei in
East Antarctica as we hear 'Copernicus' laughing—cut to a
quick succession of close-ups of stromatolite and macrofos-
sils—cut to extreme close-ups of complex igneous forms in
development—cut to an extreme wide shot, which includes a
slow-motion cutaway of 'Copernicus' dropping to the ground
and putting his opponent in an ankle lace: Huronian glaciation fuses into the Vredefort and Sudbury Basins, asteroid
impacts, and time-lapse images of Penokean and Trans-Hud-
sonian orogenies shape with terrific violence the terrain of
North America ~ fade from one microscopic close-up to another of: protists, green algae colonies in the sea, eukaryotes,
and acritarchs in combat to establish their existence—cut to
an extreme wide shot in time-lapse, including a cutaway of
'Copernicus' scoring a fall, of: Pan-African plates crumpling
and thickening to the Rodina landmass breaking into pieces ~
fade to close-ups of multi-celled animals, Ediacaran biota

flourishing in worldwide seas, trilobitomorphs, soft-jellied
creatures, the appearance of modern animal phyla, chordates,
reef-building organisms, inarticulate brachiopods, and the
perishing of Ediacaran fauna—cut to an extreme wide shot of
Gondwana strenuously emerging in slow motion, then to the
sound of crunching cartilage, cracking bones, and grunts, cut
to a quick barrage of close-ups of: invertebrates diversifying
into a multitude of types, corals, articulate orthida, nautiloids,
ostracods, conodonts, and the initial advent of green plants
and fungi on land ~ and as we hear the jeering of the crowd
crescendo, fade to a mid-shot: jawed and armored jawless fish
struggle for their individual terrain as sea-scorpions, tabulate
and rugose coral, and mollusks assert their domains—cut to
an extreme time-lapse wide shot of Caldonian orogeny in
what will become England, Ireland, Wales, Scotland, and the
Scandinavian mountains, with a cutaway of 'Copernicus' doing a belly-to-back suplex, throwing his opponent in a wide
arc, clearly maintaining a fall, a bead of his sweat dropping
into the protestor's eye—cut to slow motion time-lapse close-
ups of club mosses, horsetails, and ferns bursting into appearance, as well as trees, wingless insects, the arising of squid-like
coleoids and the decline of trilobites and armored agnaths as
the lamentations of the defeated protestor are heard ~ fade
into a cascade of wide shots of placoderms, lobe- and ray-
finned fish, and the early form of sharks dominating the seas
to large primitive trees, the first land vertebrates, and amphibi-
ous sea-scorpions flourishing amid coal-forming swamps with
cutaways of the second match beginning while lobe-finned
rhizodonts, blastoids, and spiriferida abound as trilobites

and nautiloids decline in the midst of the glaciation of East
Gondwana while winged insects suddenly radiate and the first
reptiles stake their claim of the earth—cut to an extreme wide
point-of-view shot from the moon to the landmasses of the
earth uniting into the supercontinent Pangaea, creating the
Appalachians with ferocious levels of energy as we hear the
sound of 'Lucretius' victoriously executing a double-leg take-
down and the Permo-Carboniferous glaciation concludes—
cut to close-ups of: synapsid reptiles becoming plentiful, para-
reptiles and temnospondyl amphibians wandering in their
terrain, and coal-age flora replacing gymnosperms as the first
true mosses, beetles, and flies evolve while marine life flour-
ishes in warm shallow reefs as we hear the sound of the opponent of 'Lucretius' invoking the law and commanding,
"Obey, obey!"—cut to a point-of-view shot from the moon as
95% of life on earth becomes extinct while orogenies in North
America, Europe, and Asia peter off and archosaurs dominate
the land, seizing it as their territory, and ichthyosaurs and
nothosaurs rule the oceans and the first mammals and croco-
dilia emerge, as do coral, teleost fish, and modern insect clades,
each asserting their realms—cut to extreme wide shots in
slow-motion time-lapse of Andean, Cimmerian, and Rangi-
tata orogeny as conifers and cycads abound, the first birds and
lizards claim their places, and sea urchins, starfish, and brachiopods uphold their dominions during the cracking of Pangaea into Gondwana and Laurasia as a cutaway is made of
'Lucretius' executing a grapevine and then a body throw, vigorously tossing his opponent to the ground, provoking the crowd
to cheer—cut to close-ups of: flowering plants burgeoning

along with various types of insects, more advanced teleost fish, and then, slowly, zoom out to an extreme wide shot of: Tyrannosaurs, Titanosaurs, and horned dinosaurs evolving on land while Eusuchia, Mosasaurs, and modern sharks stake their claim of the sea and primitive birds slowly supersede pterosaurs, and monotremes, marsupials, and placental mammals appear—cut to a very wide shot: Gondwana cracks and breaks up as atmospheric carbon dioxide levels significantly decrease, leading to tropical climates, while the appearance of modern plants and the diversification of mammals follow upon the extinction of dinosaurs as a wide shot cut-away of 'Lucretius' forcing his opponent into a danger position then quickly scoring a fall is fused into an extreme wide shot of Alpine orogeny in Europe and Asia as the Indian subcontinent collides with Asia and Himalayan orogeny commences ~ fade to a very wide-shot of the reglaciation of Antarctica, the formation of its ice cap, and the triggering of the Ice Age and Icehouse Earth climate while seafloor algae settles and decays, sucking in colossal aggregates of atmospheric carbon dioxide—cut to an extreme wide shot of: the aggressive formation of the Alps and the Hellenic orogeny beginning in Greece and the Aegean sea as the rapid evolution and diversification of fauna occurs along with the major evolution and dispersal of new flowering plants and mammal and bird families take recognizable form, with horses and mastodons thriving upon the earth along with grass and apes, which is accompanied by the applause of the crowd as the *agonothetai* pronounce 'Lucretius' the victor—cut to a very wide shot of: the aggressive formation of the Carpathian orogeny in Central and Eastern

Europe, the slowing of the Hellenic orogeny, and the thriving and extinction of large mammals and evolution of anatomically modern humans ~ fade to an extreme wide shot in time-lapse depicting the dawn of stone-age culture and the painting of caves and carving of stones and sculpting of figurines—cut to a very wide shot: the super-volcano of Lake Toba erupts, provoking a fierce volcanic winter that brings early man to the brink of extinction—cut to a point-of-view shot of the earth from the moon, recording the last glacial period, the rise of a dominating human civilization and formation of the Sahara, the beginning of agriculture, and the various ages of man—cut to an extreme wide shot of the eruption of Mount Tambora in 1815 and the formation of another volcanic winter—cut to an extreme close-up of six pregnant geese losing their heads to the sharp blade of Triboulet's sword as he turns to the crowd declaring:

And so we offer this gift to the protestors who, despite their backwards ways, valiantly struggled to win, for they, too, in spite of their counter claims, also long—to triumph! Have they not always longed to inherit the entire earth?

Cut to a wide shot: the protestors approach the table of the *agonothetai* and retrieve the headless geese, then bow to the victors, 'Copernicus' and 'Lucretius,' who turn to them in thanks, each responding, "*Buona fortuna*, friends!" as the midgets spray the defeated with a volley of urine and leap and hop around maniacally.

Cut to a very wide shot of the wrestling area: the kids quickly roll up the wrestling mat and push it under the *agonothetai* table as numerous women from the troupe quickly follow behind them, rolling carpets upon the ground while others trail after them dispersing flowers in their wake—cut to a mid-shot: Triboulet blows upon his three horns and then addresses 'Copernicus' and 'Lucretius':

To the victors of today's game, friends, we honor your skill and your elegance as well as your strength and courage, though, as you well enough know, victory, as all else, is not permanent, and ones greater than us will come and vanquish us—but so be it! What matters is the spirit in which we fight. As noble contestants, to you we offer a gift, and to the new epoch that is forming before us, all of which are signs of a great new dawn!

Cut to a wide shot from Triboulet's perspective of what is now the dancing space: to the clang of finger cymbals, the gentle rapping of tambours, and the clear sounding of flutes, eight women, including Aurora, who leads the group, begin dancing for the victors, a gold crown adorning the leader's braided hair, while one wears hyacinth, one myrtle and roses, one palm leaves, one a cypress crown, one a long cloak and veil, one a crown of ivy, and another a cloak embroidered with stars while the final woman sits beside the rug, accompanying the dancers on a guitar, attending to their every movement as they perform, entrancing the men with their gestures, the elegance with which they sculpt the air, carving it with their hands, each finger precisely articulated, each hand movement clear, lucid, pointed, each turn marked by grace, as they flip their veils and spin around one another, entwining and releasing themselves, breaking each embrace, inviting and repelling, independent as cats, spiraling to and fro, in silence, speaking, their lissome limbs, expressive as their eyes, stepping with vigor and strength, their feet as sculpted as their fingers, pivoting here and there, vaulting through the air as if birding they ago, their torsos swift as willows, for poised they mark the game, curving to the edge, bound yet free they glide upon an arc, winding back to salute the victors, who boldly clap their hands then come to seize the women with unreserved hunger—cut to a close-up: Aurora raises her hand to stop the men, and the women turn and pivot free of their grasp as Aurora addresses the victors:

Friends, but wait, although we honor the boldness and vigor with which you wish to receive your gifts, this is but a prelude to that which shall soon be yours—it is not the gift of which Triboulet spoke; once there were eight beatitudes, but such values have no honor here—to discount chance and contingency is to discount life and its actual mysteries; we care not for blissful rest and certainty, let alone tranquility and peace—instead, we invoke risk and danger, for the daring are those who willingly break upon secrets too hard for most to bear! In honor of the tender, innocent, puerile cruelty of chance, let us 'cast dice' and choose by them how the days and nights shall pass from here on in—Triboulet, bring out the cages!

Cut to a medium close-up: Triboulet walks to the other end of the roof, where he places two interconnected cages, both of which are covered with thick black velvet.

Cut to a mid-shot of Aurora: In each cage is an animal, but only one can be set free, for to open the door that frees one releases a mechanism that beheads the other, yet if one is not released, both will die of starvation, for they are constricted in such a way that they cannot move, nor be fed through the cage. Cut to a close-up of the cages as Triboulet removes the fabric: in the left cage resides a baby monkey, in the right, an old dove—cut to a medium close-up of Aurora: The bird before you is now essentially extinct, save for this last one, which I have kept, while many monkeys remain; but as the last of its kind, the bird has no other with which to continue its species—shall it be freed to live till old age, perhaps to die slowly, to wither away, like some *non-compos mentis* shell of itself, or would you freely end its life while it still pulses with life so that the baby monkey can learn to become what it longs to be? Your choice determines not merely whether each animal will live or die, but also the very character of the gift that you will receive.

Cut to a mid-shot: 'Copernicus' and 'Lucretius' confer, whispering to one another, wrestling the dove-monkey dialectic, turning every now and then to the cages themselves, then to the nine women, then to the giggling kids and the naked midgets sitting at the foot of the *agonothetai* table—cut to a point-of-view shot of the two victors gazing towards the judges, though it is 'Lucretius' alone who speaks: "Although we know which animal we'd set free—a freedom bound up with death, which is natural and not to be feared—if you truly wish for chance to rule, then no choice can be made by us: it is to hazard, accident, and fortune that all is to be risked."

Cut to a close-up of Aurora: And how?

Cut to a medium close-up of the victors: "With dice themselves—the roll closest to nine decides the fate!" Cut to a mid-shot: 'Lucretius' walks towards the kids, hands one of them a pair of dice—cut to a point-of-view shot of Lucretius

gazing at the kids: "Now roll for the dove." The kid rolls the
dice, which spin and tumble on the roof, then land—cut to a
close-up of 'Lucretius' announcing the number: "7." Cut to a
medium close-up of the animals as 'Lucretius' speaks: "Now
roll for the monkey!" The sound of the dice striking the roof
cuts into the silence as the dove and the monkey gaze out of
their cages at the spectacle and watch as the dice bounce, roll,
and turn on the rooftop then come to a stop, though they don't
know that their fates have just been decided but only gaze in
confusion and wonder as the kids rush towards them—slowly
turning the tight latch of one of the doors, the kids watch as it
begins to open increment by increment and a thin blade gently
scores the flesh of the one animal, then lightly penetrates it, a
spurt of blood spraying out of its neck, and turning the latch
further, the blade ruptures the animal's main artery then finally severs its head from its body as the other animal is freed
and the kids all shout, "10!" and dance about in the blood then
smear it over themselves like war paint.

   Cut to a wide shot: as the kids chase the monkey around
the roof, Triboulet rises from behind the *agonothetai* table
and addresses the victors: My friends, how bold and daring
you are! The leisure with which you let chance truly decide
your gift is an act we cannot but honor—even if it was the
dove that gained its freedom, we still would have invited you
to participate in the act of grand creation that I have planned.
I can think of no greater gift, but it requires true fearlessness
if not warlike audacity …

   Cut to a point-of-view shot and zoom into the distance:
Triboulet pivots around and faces north, then places three

horns into his mouth and produces a piercing, ferocious note in the upper register, suddenly drops to the lower, making a cacophony of deep rumbling noises, the very horns shaking and trembling on his chest as he rocks back and forth: squeals, shrieks, and guttural sounds emanate from the brass and continue for one minute, reaching an explosive peak, marked by the irruption of cymbals, parade drums, bells, and a host of percussion, all of which fall silent when Triboulet releases the horns from his mouth—in that interval of quiet, he removes a flute from the bell of his tenor saxophone, pivots back towards the victors, and facing south, creates a flowing stream of notes that sound like gentle rippling water, which culminate after 12 bars as Triboulet's helicopter lands in a field just northeast of Risus Square and he announces: Come, let us begin—the time is nigh!

Cut to an extreme wide shot from above of Risus Square and beyond, facing northwest: Triboulet, the victors, and several other men descend from the roof and run to the helicopter as Aurora and the rest of the troupe gather their belongings and pack them in the ship-car—cut to a very wide shot of the helicopter flying north above the Jordan River to Tebnine, Lebanon, with point-of-view cutaways of Triboulet scanning the landscape, from the dwindling Dead Sea to the arid deserts and the low lying mountains to the east to the highly salinized Sea of Galilee—cut to a wide point-of-view shot: at top speed, Aurora captains a hydrofoil through the Mediterranean Sea, wandering through Turkish and Greek islands, dolphins frequently rising in and out of the water as if accompanying them on their way, until she comes to the

westernmost promontory of Ikaria, where the Mediterranean
and the Aegean seas blend, and then ushers everyone to shore,
where they situate themselves on the verdant slopes and bar-
ren steep rocks and ravines of the lush green island to begin
preparing for a celebratory feast and festival in honor of the
audacious and startling creation that Triboulet and the victors are in the midst of orchestrating—cut to a series of close-
ups, mid-shots, and wide shots of the men and women of the
troupe preparing the festival area through laying out carpets,
erecting large tripods with cauldrons full of coals, building
ceremonial chairs out of oak, creating altars, hanging banners,
gathering flowers, fruits, and nuts, and building pens for the
animals, some of whose horns they gild while other animals
are oiled and receive garlands and bells—cut to a very wide
shot, the morning of New Year's Eve: Aurora is skirting the
shore line of the promontory, watching otters dive for fish as
she spies a peregrine falcon soaring above, cutting an elegant
path through the air and diving to the earth, then perching
on a crag not far from her, extending its bluish-black wings
to their limit and gently flapping then closing them, folding
its supple limbs against its body.

It is done! The creation is complete!

Cut to a close-up: Aurora blows upon a conch, sounding
it three times—cut to a wide shot: Aurora wanders along the
coast, climbing over and on top of rocks, leaping from some
like a goat, until she reaches further inland and begins running
through the oak trees as the sound of Triboulet's helicopter is
heard approaching—cut to a very wide shot: Aurora enters
the festival area, blows upon her conch, and the initial ceremo-

ny of the day begins, with the women dressed in woolen high-
girdled *chitons* that accentuate their breasts, heavy mantles
decorated with purple bands, their hair swept up and bound
by purple ribbons, jewelry adorning their necks, their faces
painted with gold or rubbed with olive oil. Some of them raise
lustral branches in the air while others carry baskets full of
grain and the men, who are dressed in *chitoniskos*, are bearing
water, both for drinking and for sharpening knives—cut to a
wide shot: Triboulet and the victors emerge from the helicopter shouting the *alalagē*, prompting Aurora to exult, draw an
arrow in her bow, and strike a target at the far end of the festival area, at last beginning the procession, which the women
lead, followed by the men, the midgets, and the kids, who are
dressed in white and crowned with wreaths. At the end of the
procession is a bull fastened with ropes, which several of the
men hold, controlling its movement as all march along to the
sound of double pipes, finger cymbals, and tambours, casting flowers in the air as the monkeys, goats, and hyenas frolic
around the hills, till the procession reaches a sanctuary where
Aurora and the three aged women await, sitting in raised chairs
in each corner of the space. After the women in the procession
sprinkle grain over the head of the bull, the men release the
animal, which runs wild, and the four women leap down from
their chairs and circle it, pacing around the majestic creature
to the wild, uproarious music of the troupe, till at last they
catch the bull and raising their sickles, in swift, balletic moves,
sweep them around the animal as if dancing with it, leaping in
the air like acrobats, then cut its throat, simultaneously raising
the *ololugē*, which the other women also pronounce while the

men sound the *alalagē*, the flames of the cauldrons rising in the air as everyone else joins in the celebration, the bull's ferocious, guttural cries dwindling in the exuberant and energetic tumult, its wine-dark blood flooding out of its body, saturating the earth as its legs kick and jerk, the spasmodic tremble of its flesh portending the shudders and quakes that will soon ripple through the flesh of the troupe at night—cut to a midshot: Aurora and the three aged women lay portions of the raw bull meat on the banquet table before Triboulet and the victors, then begin cooking the rest as the men recite passages from *Coena Cypriani*, then begin acting out episodes, all to the great amusement of the troupe, especially when Triboulet enacts the female roles, expanding upon them, intensifying the parody even more, at which point, in the midst of the ribald jocularity, he comes upon the idea of founding two entirely new feasts, announcing:

Listen, tonight, to crown our earth shattering creation, let us inaugurate two new feasts—once, at this time of the year, on this very day in fact, a feast was held in honor of the one that I once was, the Feast of the Circumcision! But what do we care for such abominations? It is erotism and gaiety that are divine. In their honor, on this momentous night, in honor of Year 0, let us instigate *The Feast of the Clitoris* and *The Feast of the Prostate*—that and that alone are how rapture will come to us my friends: through the trembling flesh! It is not transubstantiation that we seek, but ecstasy! And although rapture can be and is achieved through thought and through creation, on this night, it is through the nerves that it will be achieved. Although our creation is a radical and war-

like transvaluation, and although we offer several new directions in which to flow, all of which the world will soon come to
know, we prescribe no commandments, nor do we prescribe
doctrines, for each must create his or her own law, for there is
no such thing as *the law*—as a great madman once said, One
Law for the Lion and Ox is Oppression! If you are sick, then
find your cure, but let it not become a cure for all, though for
nearly every ill, if there is anything that we'd propose, it would
be laughter and laughter alone!

Cut to a wide shot of Aurora and the three aged women
distributing meat to all, everyone cheering in honor of the
Anno Risus and the new feasts, gnawing on joints of bull meat,
passing large vessels of wine amongst themselves, fighting
with the monkeys, who try to steal the wine, and erupting into
dances, their bodies as free, bold, and energetic as the flames
leaping from the cauldrons lining the sanctuary, which flicker
in the night, pulsing and throbbing like hearts, or dancing
stars, and to the thunderous, explosive, and frenetic blitzkrieg
of the troupe, the three aged women accompany Triboulet
and Aurora to the woods and watch as they strip one another
of their clothes and he begins the Feast of the Clitoris until
Aurora reaches a state of complete rapture and then she begins the Feast of the Prostate until he reaches a state of complete rapture, both trembling, jerking, twitching, their bodies
as spasmodic as the bull's, both howling, uttering the *ololugē*
and the *alalagē*, collapsing on the ground, whispering: We
are the *Alalagē* and the *Ololugē* … as the troupe culminates
their performance, producing a terrifying sound with their
every instrument, which resembles the earth violently tearing

open — — — — — — — — — — — — as the tone resonates in the air, the members of the troupe put their instruments down and strip off one another's clothes, join in the feasts as the fire of the cauldrons continue to burn through the night, with all eventually collapsing like the bull and chanting: We are the *Alalagē* and the *Ololugē* ~ fade out …

5 January, 0, A.R., fade in to an extreme wide point-of-view shot from the perspective of the falcon soaring over the western promontory of Ikaria: spotting its prey, Triboulet's bird begins its stoop, folding back its tail and wings, tucking in its feet, and diving with terrifying speed, seizes its enemy with its clenched feet, striking and then capturing it in mid-air and after soaring to the utter edge of the promontory, picks its prey clean, stripping every feather from it to tear and devour the raw meat as Triboulet, Aurora, and the other members of the troupe approach the surrounding rocks. Gazing up at them from his prey, the falcon watches as they remove their clothes—cut to a close-up of Triboulet's clean shaven face:

Once, I used to step into rivers, but now, I dive into seas, for diving is preferable to blessing—it is not theophanies that are to be sought, but knowledge, truth, and ecstasy. Cut to a point-of-view shot of the falcon tearing at its prey, its fierce, clear, lucid eyes ever watchful, and turning its head, the bird gazes towards the water as it hears the sound of multitudes of people diving into it …

EPIPHANY

Clay turned abject, pots shattered, clocks stopped, and lights went out, darkness suffusing and enveloping all illumination in the area as if the sun had not set but from its gravitational course been tersely broken, cast into space's outer reaches, plunging the earth into cold, dark, dark night since for the faithful the primordial *fiat* was undone. People spoke of loud bangs, sharp jolts, rolling motions, roars, and deep rumbling sounds, like nearby thunder, or approaching bullet trains, the violent rocking of the ground as it rapidly jerked in different directions, the successive jerks being of greater scope than the earlier ones, the surface of the ground vibrating visibly in all directions, as if the earth beneath was like liquid, or a mobile mass of jelly, rampant confusion seizing people as they lost their balance, the earth shaking violently, huge buildings swaying like trees in the wind as low frequency sound waves were heard but could not be localized while smoother, more monotonous sounds were reported far from the epicenters of the explosions, rapid vertical and transverse vibrations both tearing open the ground, extensive cracks appearing along the earth, though perhaps what terrified many more than anything was when they saw birds flying in the air drop suddenly, falling as if having lost their power, or as if they were instantaneously paralyzed, their delicate poise disturbed as they plummeted to the earth, but then finally recovered themselves, making many feel as if the balance of the world had been upset, that nature itself unformed, turned chaotic, which, coupled with the live streaming of Christ's decrucifixion of himself, led many to believe that the end times had actually come, though not as St. John envisioned, for never before had a monotheistic deity defected, yet the earthquake was not some vengeful ontological event, nor was it the result of natural seismic activity, at least, not entirely.

Since his return, Triboulet had been avidly studying the earth and all of its fault lines and plate boundaries, diligently analyzing sea and ocean floor as well as plate tectonic maps and satellite images of the stratifications of the earth. It was however when he learned that oil repositories were discovered off the coast of Lebanon and Israel, and then later on land in both countries, that he devised his sublime creation, for he knew that earthquakes could be invoked and that due to the intensified, vigorous, and sustained off- and on-shore drilling being done by both Israel and Lebanon over a period of 20 years, the likelihood of an earthquake occurring in a rift valley was inordinately high, especially if further provoked by acts of controlled demolition in concordance with such rapacious plundering of the earth. Over time, Triboulet began burying deep in the ground multitudes of dynamite compacted oil drums, from Tebnine to Safed to Capernaum and other places all the way to the West Bank, with heavy deposits of explosives being laid near the Sea of Galilee, Bethlehem, Hebron, the Dead Sea, then across the border in Al-Karak and other points in Jordan, and it was that intrepid venture to which Triboulet invited 'Copernicus' and 'Lucretius,' to form a creation unlike any that had ever been made on earth, one which was also an act of war against an infectious coterie of acolytes and the declaration of a multitude of new directions in which the earth could flow. Flying from destination to destination, the victors accompanied Triboulet to each point of detonation so as to calibrate the various charges. After setting the last explosive and soaring away, the men hovered off shore, waiting for the drums to ignite, not knowing whether or not their creation would form as they desired it to do, yet firm and joyous in their conviction that, at very least, something cataclysmic would occur. And so it did, the concatenation of successive explosions rippling from Lebanon to Israel to Jordan, sounding like a series of veritable atom bombs, the thick continental plate arching upwards, straining with all its power and might, pulled thin by extensional forces, fracturing into rift-shaped structures, plates pulling apart, faults developing on both sides of the rift, a magnificent rupture tearing the earth into pieces, shooting from Tebnine to Safed to Capernaum, splitting in half the Church of Beatitudes, which exploded like a piano plummeting to the earth from 2,000 feet, the rift growing ever deeper and deeper, dropping below sea level allowing ocean waters to flow in as the rupture raced southward, like a panther chasing its prey, skirting the Jordan River into Jericho, Bethlehem, and Hebron, cutting under the earth to Al Judayyidah and Al-Karak, forever altering the geographical landscape of Lebanon, Jordan, and Israel, cracking the countries into pieces, severing the West Bank in half, unforming the structure of the Sea of Galilee and the Dead Sea, creating 12 new rivers, which was Triboulet's ultimate wont and audacious creation of creations, the very work that he sought to engineer since first abdicating in his heart, bringing an end at last he hoped to biblical claims on land, and much more, instigating the gaping maw of the earth to swallow such places as if they were but pestilences the planet needed to eradicate once and for all,

for are not rivers that which tear or cleave things apart? Soaring back over the sites, Triboulet, 'Copernicus,' and 'Lucretius'
caſt from the copter white, gold, and green broadsides which
on one side contained the phrases

Still reſting? Still asleep?

The hour has come!

and which on the other side contained a map (forecaſt as far
as they could imagine the earth would reform) renaming the
territories of the earth that they had created as well as the 12
new rivers—new direćtions, Triboulet remarked, in which the
world could flow:

The Herodotus, Apuleius River, The Horace,

Aurelius River, The Galileo, Machiavelli River,

The Rabelais, The Montaigne, The Vātsyāyana,

Nietzsche River, The Einſtein and The Mandelbrot

The cataclysms however were not merely seismic but ſpiritual,
catapulting multitudes and multitudes of people into abysses,
all of them wailing and grinding their teeth, their lamenta-
tions rising in the air like the sounds of wounded animals, a
ululating chorus of pained and curséd noises, which became

prominent and pervasive once the tumult from Triboulet's creation died down. In other countries however, the wailing and grinding and lamentations were conspicuous ever since the decrucifixion. Although Triboulet, Aurora, and the troupe had inaugurated a new calendar and proclaimed the onset of Year 0, as they themselves knew perfectly well, the world was still ruled by the old calendar and it would take decades, if not far longer, for psychic structures to be entirely reconfigured; although such vigorous and total gestures had to be enacted so as to inaugurate a new epoch, they did not think in immediate terms, nor did they believe that transformations could occur with such ease, so each of their actions were crucial but specifically incremental steps in a long immeasurable chain of events that would stretch into the infinite future with the work of each new band, for they thought in millennial terms, their sense of time broad and protracted. For them, there were no panaceas, let alone instant ones. Nonetheless, the live broadcast of the abdication brought about a rupture that was primordial and sudden, as if people's souls were violently eviscerated from their bodies, for never had a god returned to abdicate and thereby unfound what was instituted in his or her name, and the act terrified many if not most believers, who cried out, *"Cursed be the day wherein I was born!"* and *"Let the stars of the twilight thereof be dark!"* and *"Why did I not give up the ghost when I came out of the belly?"* and *"Blessed are infants which never see the light!"* making cry after nihilistic cry. The event initiated mass suicides, with even priests, bishops, and nuns cutting their throats, hanging themselves, setting themselves on fire, or ending their lives in some other violent manner, for trained as they were in the art of corporal mortification, such brutality came natural to them, was an almost instinctive act or propensity that was simply activated by Christ's refutation of the

and erasure of the stigmata.

Yet, despite Triboulet's exact resemblance to the Christ, despite the fact that he actually was the Christ returned, numerous believers doubted the spectacle and denounced him as the devil incarnate, who they argued would in fact be able to take any form, to manipulate his body at will, to use matter against spirit, and when the cross was renounced, others came forth to take it up and to pronounce themselves the Christ, especially in the Americas, Korea, and the Philippines, so an inordinate number of Christ simulacrums proliferated, but lacking the resources of the troupe, the efforts of the nouveau prophets were impotent and merely local, circumscribed to small fanatical communities, who fought and argued over who was the Christ, each battling to take up the instrument and to be crucified before the other, each asserting that they were the Man of Sorrows, each scourging themselves, each impaling upon their heads razor wire crowns, for they felt that they could improve upon the crucifixion, intensify it with modern technology, each flagellating themselves with ever more sophisticated whips, which they purchased from fetish shops, along with other BDSM gear, each drinking gall, piss, and vinegar, each carrying reeds, each traversing their improved version of the *Via Crucis*, some supplementing the way with up to 30 other stations, each with a bystander yearning to have his ear cut off, each with a bystander yearning to cut off the ear, some hammering nails into their own feet, others hammering nails into their left hands while their neighbors hammered the nails into their right hands, all performing the mockery, gleefully spitting and cursing in "His" face, each calling for their own *Titulus Crucis*, with some even declaring to die to save the fallen Christ, that they in fact had surpassed the Christ in redeeming the defected Christ, and many exulting as dice were rolled and lots were cast for the seamless robe, each hungrily awaiting the final call of the cock and each dying and being removed from the †, anointed, shrouded, wept over, but none rising from the dead on the third day, nor on the fifth, nor on the seventh, prompting many to perform the resurrection and to convince others that it had occurred, for many still wanted to believe, regardless of the falsehood and even despite the fact that the Christ himself rejected the teachings founded in his name, and so they pretended that there was a resurrection and compelled others to agree that it was so, enlisting those who were still faithful to claim that they were raised from the dead, or that, miraculously, they had been healed, which many others were convinced of because the blind were able to see and the deaf were able to hear, though the healed ones didn't know that they had been abducted, put under heavy anesthesia, and operated on without their knowledge, being given bionic eyes and ears, then left in a graveyard to awaken to the miracle. And so it was, with the fanatical new sects even writing their own revised gospels, each seeking to establish the definitive gospel, each condemning other gospels as false, or corrupt, or heretical, with many savoring the role of Bishop Irenaeus more than the role of the Christ, and still others savoring the role of Paul, or Constantine, but their efforts were futile, for masses of people in the area surrounding the earthquakes leapt into Triboulet's crevices for they could not bear to live without being commanded by a god, or without having the absolute certainty of a god with which to substantiate their existence, and lacking the will and the wherewithal to command themselves, they cursed the cosmos, black holes, dark matter, and dark energy as they leapt to their death while scores of people drowned themselves in the different rivers, though most drowned themselves in The Nietzsche, hoping that they could contaminate it, but it remained the cleanest, most limpid, powerful, and pellucid river for the abyss within it simply churned and consumed whoever sought to perish there as if Scylla and Charybdis awaited such food, and on the banks of The Nietzsche laughing falcons were heard to chuckle at the spectacle while others discovered that bees proliferated along the river and that they produced the sweetest, most intoxicating and delectable honey. For aside from the nausea-drunk metaphysicians who continued to annihilate themselves, overwhelmed as they were by utter meaninglessness, by the persistent fear that if nothing was true everything would be permitted, there were many who felt truly emancipated, that clarity of some kind and degree had at last started to emerge, and they invented games after the broadcast of the abdication, with some even building enormous swings over the rivers and the crevices formed due to Triboulet's act, and it was those courageous people who discovered the bees and first cultivated and tasted their honey, and they became devoted and superior apiarists, provoking many to come from far and wide to taste of their honey while others journeyed to the new land masses to participate in the games that had been inaugurated there and to enjoy the famed swings, all of which were painted gold, white, and green and topped with pine cones. Some of the swings carried their riders just over the edges of each river or crevice, while other more enormous ones were built that traversed the entire expanse of different parts of each river, while ever more daring figures erected wires over the rivers and crevices, traversing them like tightrope dancers, and then there were those who climbed into the crevices, descending to the very depths of the earth to examine what lie beneath, and then those factions of people who erected observatories in the deserts and studied in earnest deep space, for they knew that one would never reach the *Ding-an-sich* through consciousness alone and that it was nothing but atavism to think otherwise. And aside from establishing the agon, Triboulet and Aurora announced that they would also be establishing entirely pagan educational institutions wherein one would undergo training of the mind and character as well as training of the body. In these modern gymnasiums, Greek & Latin would be mandatory once again, and the original seven liberal arts would be part of the curriculum, too, with music comprising reading and writing, counting, singing, and the playing of instruments, while clowning would be another of the arts and all of the students would be schooled in self-mastery, in learning how to become what they are, and of developing active, lively, energized, and sensual bodies. Aurora emphasized however that entry to the school would require passing through Triboulet's labyrinth, and mazes would be constructed in the vicinity of each school. In founding such places, Triboulet and Aurora sought to cultivate anew the very institutions whose decline was disastrously hastened by the conversion of Constantine and the establishment of Constantinople, a Christian city from its foundation, as the new Roman capital.

It is not salvation that mankind depends on, Triboulet announced, but nutriment! The question that we must address to ourselves is how to nourish ourselves so as to attain our maximum of strength, of *virtù* in the Renaissance style, of virtue free of moral toxicity. We are not concerned with metaphysics, but with 'physics'! We are not concerned with 'spirit' and 'soul,' but with the body and with the cosmos, with astronomy, not theology, with geology, not creationism. Since the establishment of the †, though there have been ruptures in the tyranny of that symbol and its ethics, mankind has largely been ruled by spectres and bogeymen, by pernicious concepts such as 'God,' 'soul,' 'virtue,' 'sin,' 'the Beyond,' 'truth,' and 'eternal life.' Our greatness is not to be sought in such foolhardy concepts! We are not concerned with 'big' things, but with 'small' things, with what the quintessential matters of existence actually are: — nutriment, place, climate, recreation, the whole casuistry of selfishness! These are the fundamental affairs of life, and all questions of politics, of the ordering of society and education, must be reconceived in their entirety according to the rivers that have been established—health is the ruling wisdom by which life itself teaches us to abide, not salvation of the soul: — that is a *folie circulaire*! But health is to be determined by each individual alone and the needs of his or her own body, for there is no one single type that can rule! If we are to have a motto, it will be such: To laugh at fate through life's short span is the prerogative of man.

Stepping forward, tapping his cane on the ground as he emerged from the distance, not having heard the speech, an old blind man addressed Triboulet and pleaded, "Are you not the Christ? The savior of mankind? Are you not He?"

I am *Tri-bou-let*, the decrucified one enunciated, laughing, not a *cré-tin* let alone a *chré-ti-en*.

"What? Is this a parable?"

Bad jokes are better than no jokes, old man!

"Do you not still heal people? Will you not perform a miracle for us?"

What need have you of miracles?

"I am blind."

There are many people with eyes who cannot see.

"Do you not pity me? Have you no mercy? I have come long and far, walked many miles to find you."

If you want to be cured, visit a doctor, not a jester, juggler, and band leader.

"A pox on physicians! *A pox!*"

What? You trust in miracles, but not in medicine? Old man, are you that paradox of paradoxes—a *Christian scientist*? I would not want you for a father!

"Did not God anoint you with the Holy Ghost so that you could do good and heal by your stripes? I am oppressed of the devil; I am blind—*heal me!*"

And if I were to cure you, would you not look upon this world with your restored eyes and curse it as those of your kind, longing as you do for other worlds, worlds of comfort and tranquility and peace, worlds founded on vengeance against reality? With your renewed eyes, would you not be as blind as you are now, nothing but an inverse cripple? Oppressed of the devil? Ha! It is not your sight that needs to be restored, old man, but your reason! *Cura te ipsum!*

"Heal me, fool! Heal me! The devil has taken hold of my eyes."

What swamp did you emerge from, you funny old tadpole? I do not believe in miracles but in acts of creation! Love your suffering, old man—it might be that which makes you who you are.

"Cruel and evil fiend! You are not the Christ! Repent! The time and the hour shall come! Repent, O deceiver! *Repent!*"

As the blind man castigated Triboulet, brandishing his cane like a sword and shouting, "*Redeem us! Take up thy cross! Save us from dark matter! Restore the stigmata! Save us from dark energy! Take up thy cross!*" he who was no longer He exploded into a fit of laughter and seized the old man and pretended to heal him, laying his hands on him, commanding the devil to leave his body, mumbling prayers and incantations in Aramaic, but the blind man's sight did not return and touching Triboulet's face with his right hand, the afflicted one looked at him with his fingers, caressing his face, feeling its contours, running his hand over Triboulet's head and through his hair, taking the hand of he who was no longer He and feeling for the stigmata, which, once he realized were absent, backhanded Triboulet across the face furiously, making the redeemed savior laugh uproariously, thereby infuriating the blind man, who struck the laughing one with his cane and cursed, "Take up thy cross! Devil! Take up thy cross!" Seizing the cane, Triboulet tore it from the blind man's grasp, then executed a gut wrench, gently rolling the old man over his torso onto his back and pinning him to the ground, exulting: *Take up thy blindness, atavist!* As Triboulet held the man on the ground, he started tickling him, touching, prodding, stroking, and lightly caressing different areas of his body to find the most sensitive, turning his fuming into chuckles, albeit dark and angry ones, then called other members of the troupe to hold him down as the kids ran forward and surrounded him, joining in the act, mercilessly tickling the man's arm pits, sides, and feet till he twitched and jerked under their hands, his body trembling, pain and pleasure intermingling, the chortles growing more uncontrollable, his limbs spastic, twisting under their hold as from his contorted face burst high-pitched laughs, between which he kept trying to choke out the word "*heal*," but when he managed to utter it the kids would only intensify the tickling, digging their fingers into his body till tears started flowing from out the sightless ducts of the fulminating one, and they echoed him, shouting: HEAL! HEAL! HEAL! giggling maniacally as they did so, then stripping him of all his clothes, they took feathers and tickled the soles of his feet, his armpits, the inner recesses of his thighs, and other parts of his body, which was particularly sensitive, then soaked his feet in salt water, attracting the goats, who started licking his feet until they were clean of the salt, after which the kids would soak his body parts with salt water again and again, and the goats would continue lapping the salt from his feet and arm pits and even thighs and genitals until the blind man convulsed violently, his body jerking and contorting and lurching as if jolted with electricity, which terrified the goats; as they reared away from him, he died in a spasmodic fit of laughter, the kids exclaiming: CURATUS! when his body finally ceased moving.

After constructing a funeral pyre, the blind man's body was set aflame and cremated near the banks of the Nietzsche River, but as it started burning, Triboulet, Aurora, and the troupe wandered into the distance with their ship-car, playing upon their instruments, sounding a funeral dirge in honor of the dead man, and as they continued to meander into the new territory, aimlessly drifting about, they discovered a church that had survived the earthquake and peering through its windows, saw that a mass was being conducted, but silently, with the preacher's sermon displayed on a computer screen. When Triboulet blew upon one of his piercing whistles, no one seemed to hear the sound, but it was not because the congregation consisted entirely of the deaf. After learning that the troupe often and generally took hold of people through their music, the congregation decided to protect themselves against its possible influence through impacting their ears with heavy-duty wax, but they were not aware that it was not the sound of the music alone which affected, influenced, and transformed people, but the very vibrations emanating from the instruments, thus there was no safeguard against it, not even the deaf were fortified against its power, which, though they were not yet aware of it, the congregation would soon experience to their incredible horror when, after having surrounded the church, the troupe erupted into one of their most volatile and ferocious musical weapons. As the congregation was celebrating the baptism of Jesus in the Jordan River, each of them began to quiver, twitching as if their bodies were suffering from some kind of malady, which intensified as the troupe continued sounding their music, and the congregation felt increasingly devoid of control of their bodies as they began involuntarily clenching their hands and raising and lowering their arms, bending their knees, some even shouting or moaning, which made them think that the Holy Ghost was taking possession of them, and they were nearly convinced it was so when many of them started feverishly crying, but when the priest began drooling, his eyes deviating, his head whipping from side to side, they were no longer certain it was God that was visiting them, and when the priest tore off his clothes and leapt around wildly, almost hurdling from the altar with the velocity of an animal, it was not the Holy Ghost that they thought was entering them, but when they started to each see brightly colored spots, lines, and other shapes, when they could suddenly taste forms and smell colors and their eyes blinked violently and their vision deteriorated, their thought processes ceased and they tore off their clothes and danced as did the priest, all of them leaping about with abandon until finally collapsing and passing out after their bodies went into epileptic fits as Triboulet and the troupe burst into the church when their composition reached its climax, which they sustained for thirty-five minutes, rocking back and forth, trembling themselves, the muscles in their necks feverishly pulsing as the music reached its final frenetic crescendo and their drenched bodies glistened with sweat, the sounds of their myriad instruments dissipating in an illuminating crash as Triboulet enunciated one of his triple horn tones, splintering the stained glass windows of the house of worship.

Once they carried the bodies of every member of the congregation into the ship-car, they set the church aflame and watched it burn to the ground as they proceeded back to the blind man's funeral pyre, dreaming of quiet and wide, expansive places for reflection, buildings and sites that would altogether give expression to the sublimity of thoughtfulness, surroundings in which there are no gods but in which we ourselves are translated into stone and plants, so as to permit us to take walks in ourselves when we stroll through such buildings and gardens, buildings in which breathing without the suffocating influence of malodorous incense would be possible, buildings completely free of all supramundane intercourse, buildings evoking physics, not metaphysics!

When they reached the river, the body, as Triboulet dubbed him, of the tadpole, was completely incinerated, and as its ashes fell to the ground, the troupe carried the bodies of the members of the congregation to the shore of the river, for they were still unconscious. While they slept, the troupe constructed an enormous scaffolding, so high in fact that it reached the clouds, for they were low lying that day, and after disguising it with mirrors and lights, Aurora climbed to its peak and donned a flowing white robe, giant fake beard and long gray hair while someone else from the troupe donned a St. John the Baptist costume and Triboulet donned a Christ costume, then walked to the bank of the Nietzsche River while the rest of the troupe donned angel costumes and took different positions around the locale, establishing a dynamic and painterly *mise en scène*.

The sound of the *salpinx* having scored the air several times, the members of the congregation at last awoke, but not because they heard the tone of the trumpet calls, but because they felt them. Since the heavy-duty wax they impacted their ears with hardened within their auditory canals making them entirely deaf, they watched the spectacle before them as if it were a live silent film, as if a portal in history had opened, transporting them back in time, or as if they were dead; they were not sure: gazing in terror and trembling with fright, they looked up and saw God the Father speaking through the clouds, extending his hand towards the earth and exhorting to the people below, God the Son being baptized in the river and gazing up towards his heavenly father, and God the Holy Spirit in the shape of a bird (Triboulet's falcon painted white) descending from heaven and alighting on Triboulet's shoulder, yet despite the size, shape, and astounding speed of the falcon, the congregation still believed it was a dove ... Prostrating themselves before the scene, they wept as the cherubim (the midgets in disguise) sang, which they could see from how they opened and closed their mouths in unison, all of them radiant and awe-inspiring, effulgent halos shimmering above their heads, a lighting trick achieved by the troupe members,

who were creating such dramatic, holy effects through ingenious stagecraft. When the mirrors concealing the scaffolding
cracked and tumbled to the ground and God fell from the
clouds into the river, the congregation thought that the very
sky was being rent in half, just as had the temple curtain on
the day that the Christ was crucified, and they watched in silent horror as they saw God drowning, or so they believed,
and were horrified when the river suddenly, almost straight-
way, turned blood red and they were not sure if the Christ had
turned the river into wine, or if the river was suffused with the
blood of the dead God (it was another lighting effect), but it
was the wild laughing Christ that astounded them most, for as
he emerged from the river with the head of what they thought
was God, along with the insects, the monkeys, goats, and hyenas were released from the ship-car and came rushing to the
banks of the river, howling, yelping, screeching, bleating, and
noising each in their varied manners, sending the congregation into cataleptic fits, for they thought that the world was
ending, that creation itself had at last been vanquished and
chaos would soon swallow the entire cosmos, suck it out of
itself and into oblivion.

As the congregation lay trembling on the ground, spittle
forming in the corners of their mouths, their eyes flipping into
the backs of their heads, Aurora emerged from the river, sans
beard, wig, and long flowing robe, which she quickly ripped
off as she swam through the river, and stood on the shore
naked, bursting into guffaws at the jest she and the troupe had
pulled off, though, as many of their jests, it was done to convince through action and experience what the faithful could

never discern through logic alone, for it is through seduction that believers come to knowledge. Delighting in the new water flowing through Triboulet's creation, Aurora urged the entirety of the troupe to enter it, and so they did, diving into it from the shore, swimming across it, savoring the sensation of the water flowing over their bodies and simply playing around, gleefully frolicking in the river as the animals and the kids lined the bank, watching the troupe as if they were animals.

When Triboulet emerged from the water, three men in the archaic guise of sages bearing gifts approached him, each of them desiring to question him, to ask of him something, but when they motioned to speak, Triboulet did not permit them to and told them that if they wished to pose a question to him, they must do so to him alone, whispering their query into his ear. Startled more by his nakedness than by his stipulation, the men were silenced, but obeyed and the troupe watched from the river as the first of the men approached Triboulet and whispered in his ear. Turning from him abruptly, he who was no longer He walked to the bank of the river in silence, then taking hold of one of the goats, tickled and tickled the animal until it started bleating, its eerie smile emerging across its face as it tossed its head to and fro, making Triboulet laugh, then sit down beside the goat to continue playing with it. After waiting a long time, the second man realized that Triboulet was not going to return to where they were and after approaching, he bent down and whispered a question into Triboulet's ear, causing he who was no longer He to stare deeply into the man's eyes, then to raise his open palms to the man's face. Standing up, Triboulet somersaulted away from the archaic sage, gracefully flipping his body along the bank of the river and landing before a troop of monkeys, who leapt up and down at his antics, performing their own somersaults, leaps, and other acrobatic feats. Taking hold of one of the monkeys, Triboulet tickled and tickled it until the animal giggled and shrieked excitedly, laughing as it smiled and leapt about, prompting Triboulet to join the animal, which horrified the questioner, who found his antics immoral and unconscionable. Lunging at Triboulet, the third man struck him with his staff several times and commanded him to cease with his frivolities, clothe himself, and answer their questions at once. When the third man threw his cloak at Triboulet, he who was no longer He caught the raiment and lifting it above his head, swung it about, dancing with it in circles, which astonished the man, who ran toward Triboulet to strike him with his staff again, but Triboulet threw the raiment into the air, deflected the blow, knocked the man to the ground and catching the old fabric, began whipping him with it, driving him to the bank of the river as if a bullfighter, flipping the fabric around him with *élan*, then twirling it above his own head, spinning ever faster and faster, so fast indeed that his body seemed to blur and almost vanish. Gazing in terror at the sight, the attacker was immobile, struggling to perceive the figure before him, who he thought was the devil, but the dust Triboulet stirred up created a cloud that obscured him entirely and so the third man could not see the jester of jesters any longer, nor could anyone else, but as he rose from the ground, suddenly, he felt the full power of Triboulet, who seized the man, putting him in a body lock, forcefully slamming him to the ground, pinning him with terrifying velocity as if possessed of the force of a panther. Holding the burly man squarely on the ground, his back absolutely flush with the earth, Triboulet bent his ear to the man's lips and waited for him to pronounce his question, which the man at first refused, attempting to break free from Triboulet's grasp, which he who was no longer He loosened simply to amuse himself, and as the man attempted to escape the hold, Triboulet executed a grapevine again and again, turning the man over and over and over till he was bruised and delirious, then scored yet another fall, squarely pinning the confused man's body to the earth again and bending down once more, waited, holding the man to the ground for three minutes as his face grew red and his limbs twitched in violent revolt … At last, Triboulet felt his lips moving, whispering the question, which he sputtered out, barely enunciating it, the veins in his arms throbbing as if they were going to explode. Releasing the man, he who was no longer He rose from the ground, at which point the enraged man leapt at Triboulet, but he who was no longer He spun around his attacker and knocked him to the earth once more, striking certain pressure points so as to render him immobile. Diving into the river, he who was no longer He swam to the depths and remained there for such a lengthy duration that no one was sure whether he was actually going to emerge or not, but he soon did, his hands coming out of the water first as he reached the other shore, then climbed out of the river, the water glistening on his muscular and powerful body as he walked towards a group of hyenas and started caressing them, petting them, rubbing their bodies, then tickling them till they started leaping at Triboulet, emitting their high-pitched siren-like laughs, which echoed across the river as he who was no longer He laughed with the hyenas, so perfectly in harmony with them that they thought he was a hyena and not human.

Forever after, that day was known as The Day of Fires and of Laughter, for while the rest of the troupe dove again and again into the river, at other points around the world, different factions of the troupe exulted:

Raze the sanctuary!

Burn it on down!

as they set flame to scores and scores of churches, chapels, synagogues, and mosques and the fire from each of them lit up the sky in every city in the world, an event that he who was no longer He had orchestrated to coincide with the overturning of the epiphany. From Istanbul to Jerusalem, Rome, and Mecca, the skies were entirely new, as clear and fresh as never before, awaiting the vision of an altogether new architecture commensurate with the philosophy of the future.

LENT

After the burning of the churches, chapels, synagogues, and mosques around the world, an event preceded in each place by the deployment of the same volatile and ferocious musical weapon used in what was formerly Israel by Triboulet and his troupe, the ashes of each building were collected and placed in large clay *lekythoi* and then lightly blended with mead. Once the mixture was ready, at the site of each clearing, people congregated so as to be covered in the ashes, which were not applied to their foreheads but to the entirety of the body of every participant after they stripped off their clothes, yet the ritual was not enacted in order to express sorrow—it was a joyous and celebratory act accompanied by bursts of giggling and laughter, and if anyone expressed remorse, sadness, or grief over the incineration of the houses of worship, or tried to confess to what they believed was some transgression, the kids applying the mixture tickled the culprit until it was no longer possible for the person to speak and they were over-come by spasms of uncontrollable laughter, which vanquished the word, engulfing speech in its boisterous cacophony, which was not only vocal, but physical, a cacophony of trembling and twitching limbs through which laughter reverberated like an omnipresent sound wave. And so for the entirety of the day, in nearly every city in the world, kids dressed in jester costumes were provoking sustained peals of laughter not only in those who persisted in repeating archaic and outmoded sacraments, but in everyone they applied the mixture to, and once all of the ashes were rubbed into bodies, the ground from which they were taken was tilled and turned over till the soil was a soft, rich, almost wet black. In that clean and fertile ground, in

that moist living matter, as they laughed, the entirety of their
naked bodies covered in ashes, including their faces, those par-
ticipating in the ritual planted multitudes of orchid seeds, and
to commemorate the day and the seed planting, at every site
poles were fixed in the ground, and upon them, long purple,
gray, and red banners were flung, streaming boldly in the sky, a
declaration of but another aspect of the dawn that Triboulet
had envisioned, emblematized in the image on each banner
of a laughing monkey wearing a crown with a *lekythos* beside
him, which contained a painting of the three aged women—
one holding a beehive, one an orchid, and the third a baby
minotaur, while above the jug was a dancing flame.

As the banners snapped in the breeze like sails proudly
cracking at sea, everyone danced around the newly cultivated
ground, energized and intoxicated by the mead soaked ashes,
which seeped into their pores the more they sweat, abandon-
ing themselves to the irresistible and primitive rhythms of the
troupe as they learned to dance and to fly, soaring, even if but
temporarily, and even if only over short distances, from the
ground as if birds, though none of them could reach the velocity levels of Triboulet, whose whirling abilities were astounding, but they continued to strive for greater and greater heights,
tempting gravity, testing their bodies, experimenting with
themselves in entirely new ways, burning down encrustations
within themselves, destroying antiquated psychic structures
that were the internal form of the physical structures that had
already been destroyed by Triboulet and his troupe. With the
near complete elimination of the concrete aspects of the virus-
es that had invaded them and taken shape in their bodies as if

equally permanent structures, many people were emancipated as never before, freed from bonds they could not previously separate themselves from, for they saw them as absolute, if not universal and true, not bonds, but actualities that abided no questioning. What devastated them even more, but in a liberating sense, divesting them of their beliefs and thus releasing them from the primitivism that made their minds and bodies into petrified objects, was the act of the decrucifixon, for it was more incisive, powerful, and shattering than any rational argument or reasoned polemic, despite the force and unerring lucidity evident in both. Upon witnessing the live streaming of the abdication of the Christ, including the removal of the nails, the crown, and the closing and erasure of the stigmata, many people were paralyzed, struck as if with bullets in the spine, but still conscious; eviscerated, but endowed anew with organs, as if feeling their organs for the very first time, sensing their very growth, development, and operation, as if becoming the first ever human being awakening on earth, not the early form of man, but the first *homo sapien*, as if a star traversing the sky, a sensation intensified to an astonishing degree when they witnessed the shaving of His beard, the cutting of His hair, and the cremation of the body, of his refusal of divinity, of his dying as a man, which made them feel like stars falling to earth and plunging into the sea, diving to the very bottom of the waters and hitting absolute ground, a sensation of power, of strength, of cleanliness, of limpidity, of beauty, of an intoxicating voluptuousness as they blended into the molten core of the earth, suffused with a multiplicity of elements, a plethora of dimensions, *sans* the metaphysical. In reenacting the event themselves, in proceeding through all of its stages, of imagining themselves as crucified beings, meditating upon the event, and then refusing the cross and the promise and the curse against existence, and dying, experiencing the incineration of their flesh and bones as nothing but flesh and bones, they were freed, a process aided by their patient, diligent, and prolonged study of Lucretius, as well as of Erasmus's criticism of the Vulgate and Valla's analysis of the 'Good Book.'

It was the reenactment of Triboulet's birth however that was equally powerful and liberating, for when they performed it themselves, they were born anew; not with the false stain of sin, but with laughter, just as Triboulet, as laughing joyful beings who embraced pain and suffering as natural aspects of existence, with the full consciousness of there being no end to time, of the erasure of all apocalyptic thought, a point of strength reached through their meditating upon one of the new rivers or directional flows set forth by Triboulet. But as they danced around the moist soil, the rhythms of the drums taking hold of them, new images forming in their minds and displacing the archaic ones, they kept thinking of salted ribs, and Aurora's counsel on the divinity of sodomy and of the sanctity of the flesh took hold of them, and they meditated upon one of the other rivers that had been created anew and on the refusal of procreation in honor of the earth, and the meditation was not merely cognitive, but physical, a flesh-thinking, a trembling of limbs, and their bodies palpitated with sensations, pulsing like the ivy upon the mast of Triboulet's ship-car, compelling them to seize one another's ash painted forms and to intertwine and connect like fractals, to form not Herakle-

otic knots, but labyrinthine passageways, weaving into one another like cool fills or weft yarns floating over warp yarns, then
breaking apart and clashing, struggling, battling, playing like
lynxes, tempting and teasing, enticing and seducing, dominating, overpowering, surrendering, conquering, then reforming, enacting The Feast of the Clitoris and The Feast of the
Prostate, warp yarns floating over weft yarns, bodies flowing
together seamlessly, creating an even sheen, the flesh lustrous,
silky, hot, warping and wefting, fusing into fascinating new
and complex shapes, arcing out like lengthy archipelagos, fracturing and splintering off like tectonic plates, fragmenting into
pieces, then reforming again, weaving and winding into other
unforeseeable patterns, creating a frenzied orgiastic mass of
limbs, lips, and organs till becoming one unified, interlock-
ing erotic entity, like the *rota fortunae*, wildly spinning and
spinning and spinning, producing ever new and unpredictable
changes and variations, the wheel saturated with an amalgam
of viscous fluids cut with sweat, rocking and rumbling on its
axle, like a train barreling along tracks never before traveled
upon, not knowing the direction of the rails, not knowing
if the earth beneath may move or bump them, and as the
wheel rolled, spinning with ever greater velocity, force, friction,
heat, noise, its whole form rattling, its axle burning, smoking,
aflame—BOOM! it explodes, the spokes and fellies breaking apart in wild spastic jerks, pieces diverging into sundry
directions, a din-like chorus of cries, moans, shouts, and unrestrained caterwauls, an ecstatic wave streaming through the
pores, muscles, bones, and marrow of all, who, as they savored
the sensations pulsing through their corpuscles, ruminated on

the monkey-dove dialectic and the ingenious response given by 'Copernicus' and 'Lucretius,' thinking of the *frisson* they must have experienced when watching the dove's head be severed from its body, cascading to the ground like a swollen lychee, the blood freely spurting from out its neck while the kids laughed, frolicking about with the monkey, wondering as they did about the power of dice, of how, despite their minuscule proportion, those seemingly innocuous objects were rather formidable, commanding enough to decide life and death, to bestow the gift of freedom, which was fraught with unsettling dangers of its own, dangers however that one had to relish, to countenance with the wherewithal of warriors. It was the strange, unnerving power of laughter that most startled them however, and the profound way in which laughter could be deployed as a weapon, a point they experienced with considerable force when Triboulet performed the *Coena Cypriani*, and they remembered it with great delight, discussing the inventiveness of the parody and the radical freedom with which it was staged, and in their naked state, the ashes almost entirely sexed from their bodies, they enacted the *Coena Cypriani*, each taking on a different role, performing a parody that was even more stinging, brutal, blasphemous, and liberating, one which ended in a supper of ribs and corn and fruits, and the recitation of the oracular fragments of Heraclitus, at the end, all chanting together in unison: war is common, strife is justice, and all things happen according to strife and necessity.

The next morning, various factions of people in countries around the world were seen burning calendars in the streets, petitioning for the removal of religious iconography and expressions from all forms of currency, as well as for the removal of such from houses and courts of law, state buildings, and educational institutions, while further alterations were called for in history and other books, so as to end once and for all the tyranny over time enacted by the former empire, a tyranny almost atomistic in nature, for it infiltrated the structure and organization of western time itself, from the numbering of years to the structure of months and days and the scheduling of holidays, with many people refusing to recognize any longer even birth years, which they found arbitrary assignations, questioning whether it was 2033, the second year of Olympiad 702, or Year 0, with others radically departing from Triboulet's designation of Year 0 and proposing that the calendar should be based either upon the actual age of the earth—as precisely as it can be calculated—while yet another faction of people proposed that it begin from the onset of the current species of humans since the calendar pertains to nothing but human endeavors and has no significance or relevance to the cosmos or the earth, but some protests ensued, with objections voiced that the propositions made for recasting the calendar were of little significance and consequence; they were even ridiculed, seen as stupid and laughable inconveniences and were derisively mocked, but the mockery was countered and neutralized when Aurora leapt before the indifferent throng and asserted with piercing fervor: Nothing matters more than that an already mighty, anciently established and irrationally recognized custom should be once more confirmed by persons recognized as rational: it thereby acquires in the eyes of all who come to hear of it the sanction of rationality itself! All respect to your opinions! But such customs must be combatted at every turn, lest we continue to be infiltrated by poisons that we have been fighting to inoculate ourselves against for ages! A holiday, now nothing but a day of leisure to many, is no mere harmless event, but imbued with millennia of weight: ethics, values, morals, even—murders! *Do you know how much blood has been spilt to establish each holiday?* How many wars fought?! How many opponents conquered?! And they claim to be the arbiters of peace!

Displaying between two fingers a slightly reddish seed that resembled a single but hard, lacquered oat, Aurora held the object aloft and loudly whispered: All those customs that we blithely affirm are but insignificant to many, supposedly of little impact and force, like this seed, but when such minuscule things take root, beware! for they can grow to incredible heights and widths, lasting for thousands of years, towering over us like unbreakable monoliths. The affirmation of every irrational custom only leads to the production of *moral sequoias*; once rooted, they are harder and harder to completely deracinate. To topple them is to topple millennia. Combat is best; war is necessary!

Stepping forth, Aurora took up an *épée* and thrust at the air with it, striking directly above her as she shouted: *En garde!* scoring the air with the weapon, spinning round and round as if carving an enormous body to pieces, and those watching were astounded by the elegance and precision of her dancing attack, and blood almost seemed to drip from the air as she exclaimed: Let the firmament tumble! Clear the air! Set the calendars aflame! Let us reconceive time; form the world anew! Unroot the moral sequoias!

And so the troupe wandered for forty days through the streets, ruminating on mountains, engaging in concourse with the earth, ſtudying flora and fauna like botaniſts, washed in continuous rain, observing the tributaries Triboulet formed flowing on and on and on, others wandering through the new regions he cut and shaped, inſtigating people to conceive anew their relationship to the surrounding lands, which were now nameless, while the troupe sought to further deterritorialize the earth, calling for the abolition of all ſtates and fatherlands, diving in the waters, engaging in conteſts, polemics, and games, feaſting, taking up new vices, building labyrinths and swings around the world, reading from the books of the five rings, ſtudying geology and deep time, and eſtablishing seasons of ecſtasy.

In the midſt of the general tumult and transformation, many wondered where Triboulet was, eſpecially the U.N. and the E.B.I., for his absence was conſpicuous, if not an indication of yet some new cataclysm in the offing. Although the troupe's aċtivities could be tracked and observed more readily, Triboulet was laſt seen descending into the heart of the earth, scaling one of the many crevices that his explosion formed, retreating, it seemed, from the ſtorm that he created, taking refuge amongſt the apparently permanent rock, recognizing that even no chain of mountains or ocean is eternal, retreating, it seemed, from the troupe, learning to see himself and humanity more and more as nothing but ſpecks of duſt in the voluminous hiſtory of the planet, learning to love impermanence, to know that the only laws that govern us are those that govern quasars and pulsars—indeed, in the atomic nuclei of his body,

38

in its quarks and electrons, Triboulet knew that traces of the Big Bang existed, that he, as all others, was but an infinitesimal iota of the primordial atom and nothing more. *Father?* But as he descended into the earth, and as the troupe circumnavigated its surface, to the astonishment of many, new sects started to arise in the deserts and backwaters of the world, with nouveau prophets interpreting Triboulet's earthquake as the one prophesied of in Revelations, the earthquake "so violent that nothing like it had ever happened in human history." And they saw him not as the true Christ—who they claimed newly appeared to them in the desert, actually descending on a cloud, not arriving by helicopter, though some heard that the so-called apparition of the real Christ was actually Triboulet on a *Deus ex machina*—but as Satan loosed from his prison, come out to seduce the nations in the four quarters of the earth, for, asserted the prophets knowingly, "did not he muster them for war? Are not he and his minions marching over the breadth of the land and laying siege to the camp of God's people and the city that he loves?" Whoever—or whatever he was, others believed that he was simply on the lam, for bounties were put upon his head by the U.N. and the E.B.I., who declared him the most wanted criminal in the world, and many feared that he was descending to the center of the earth in order to detonate it, to spur a cataclysm far more monstrous and horrific than the one that he had already given birth to, a cataclysm that would infinitely surpass the spectacle of the atomic bomb. But because the troupe proliferated to such an astonishing degree, "manifesting," said the Great Sovereign Body of the Joint Chiefs of Staff of the U.S. Government, "like an epidemic of

violent overgrown maggots," it wasn't clear where Triboulet
might have been, on what continent, at what ocean or sea, on
what mountain, or in what cave or crevice. The troupe proved
so ingenious at evading capture, too, for since their music could
affect people from considerable distances, whenever they were
descended upon, or were about to be, those in the vicinity of
their sound waves, which they projected into the surrounding
circumference whenever being pursued, were seized by their
music, a force against which no antidote had been developed,
and they were rendered helpless, falling into furious ecstatic
spasms, only to awake disoriented and altered, something in
their constitution having undergone transformation.

During Triboulet's absence, while his troupe was wandering about the world, a faction of stalwart and formidable
monks appeared in what to them was still Israel, and they
monked through the severed country, swinging censers and
offering consolation to those stricken by Triboulet's antics,
pitying the downtrodden and the despairing, who could not
bear to live without a god, and they condemned Triboulet and
what they called his works as mere worldly frivolities and reassured the weary and crestfallen that God did in fact still exist,
and they soothed the believers, chanting

> Kýrie, Rex genitor ingenite, vera essentia, Eléison.
> Kýrie, luminis fons, rerumque conditor, Eléison.
> Kýrie, qui nos tuæ imaginis signasti specie, Eléison.
> Christe, Deus formae humana particeps, Eléison.
> Christe, lux oriens per quem sunt omnia, Eléison.
> Christe, qui perfecta es bǎlatro, Eléison.

Kýrie, Spiritus vivifice, vitæ vis, Eléison.
Kýrie, Utriqusque vapor in quo cuncta, Eléison.
Kýrie, inrideo scelerum et largitor gratitæ quæsumus
propter nostras offensas noli nos relinquere,
O consolator dolentis animæ, Eléison.

As the meaninglessness of a world without a god was too exacting for many to bear, the sudden appearance of the monks
incanting their *Kýrie, eléison* was a profound and unexpected
healing salve to those too impotent to commit suicide but too
powerless to live according to their own dictums. When the
prayer was heard, many people wept, and they fell to their
knees pleading for forgiveness, for they had forsaken their
God, had thought in fact that He had forsaken them, and
they felt once again that they had failed in their faith and were
shamed at their appalling weakness, which they sought to
atone for by taking up hair shirts and crops, mortifying their
flesh, calling out, "we deny ourselves, we take up the cross anew,
we follow the living Christ," but the monks did not respond,
only listened to their utterances, observing them like scientists
as the delirious continued to wail and moan, screaming out
their anguish as if to reinforce their beliefs through ferocity,
barking, "*It is the flesh, the flesh to which we have fallen prey. I
chastise my body and bring it into subjection,*" others vehemently
crying, "Remember, 'If you live according to the flesh you will
die, but if by the Spirit you put to death the deeds of the body
you will live,'" as if to reassure God that they had not forgotten
the tenets of their faith, thinking that, if the monks witnessed

the veracity of their piousness, they would be saved and heaven would not be closed to them. But as the monks continued to gaze upon them in silence, they felt admonished, rebuked even, which made them increase the intensity of their mortifications as they recalled how God rebuked even the most faithful, one believer shouting with such violence that his face was inflamed, the veins in his neck bulging, his eyes straining from their sockets as if afflicted with proptosis: "Put to death what is earthly in you: fornication, impurity, passion, evil desire, and covetousness, which is idolatry. *Idolatry!*" he repeated, punctuating the air with his fists, "*Idolatry!*" and, as if to better his brethren, another came forward to demonstrate what superior devoutness was to the monks, cursing, "In my flesh I complete what is lacking in Christ's afflictions, *I complete!* for the sake of His body, that is the Church. *I complete! In my flesh!*" while yet another advanced, clutching at the robes of the monks, wanting to surpass all of the other believers with his passion, but when the monks knocked him to the ground, he rose before them, tore off his shirt, displayed himself, cut his flesh with glass shards, fuming, "And those who belong to Christ Jesus *have crucified the flesh with its passions and desires, crucified the flesh. Crucified!!!*" digging the shards deeper and deeper into his body as if trying to carve it away, as if to strip himself of flesh in order to be spirit alone and nothing but pure, absolute spirit.

The monks seemed immune to these vicious displays of faith, which perhaps they found grotesque, no one was sure, but they monked on, incanting the prayer as they wandered toward "Jerusalem," gathering more and more acolytes, many of whom were incredibly fearful, but who watched the monks from afar, especially since others in the street mocked them, imitating their penitent gestures, astounded by their irrationality, by their seemingly willful blindness, by the fact that, even with the very return of the Christ and with his decrucifixion and refusal of the cross, people still believed, and they called at them: Even if God did not exist, you would invent him, for illusions were to them more important than truth, while others rejoined: God's only excuse is that he does not exist—*that's why you invented him!* while still others affirmed: God is dead! And we have killed him, and: I found a rat in the holy core! and: A new dawn has come—it is Year 0! The Anno Risus, not the Anno Domini! while scores of kids and midgets came running towards the monks with handfuls of wet soil, which they threw at them as they chortled, pelting the recidivists with dirt with unrestrained glee, but the monks ignored the attacks and continued singing, marching devotedly to their destination, which the people finally realized was Golgotha, a site which survived Triboulet's creation, indicating to many that perhaps he was not the Christ, for how except by miracle would the site survive a cataclysm as monstrous as his, how except as a signifier of the everlasting veracity of the crucifixion, which God sought to preserve so as to reveal that he remained in their presence and that Triboulet was but a subterfuge, a ruse sent by God through the prompting of Satan, making each of those who still believed see themselves as Job, that God was now casting everyone in the role of Job for the world was actually soon to come to an end and He wanted to know who was and who was not truly faithful, who was to be set aside as a sheep, who as goat, but through the most exacting test of all, through the total rescinding of his Son, through the cancellation of the crucifixion, and they reassured themselves by repeating that "about that day and hour no one knows, not even the angels in heaven, not even the Son; no one but the Father alone," which many of them interpreted as implying that God would eventually rescind his Son, "for if even the Son was not aware of the day and the hour of the final judgment, then what did it matter if He decrucified himself? Did He not even renounce the Father when on the cross? O, how terrifying silence is," they thought, "how abominable, how crucifying—but God's silence is not God's absence: — only *something* can be silent," they rejoiced, "and there is something, not nothing, there is something! It is the silence of the absent but ever present deity! Hosanna to the Highest! Hallelujah!" they rejoiced, "Hallelujah!"

Were not the acts to which all were witness signs that the end was in fact near, that the prophets were right, that the earthquake signified the actual forthcoming wrath? That the time was in fact upon them, that it was as nigh as never afore, so frighteningly, appallingly, terribly nigh? Shuddering, many prostrated themselves at the feet of the monks, kneeling with prodigious force as if they wanted to kneel into the very ground and bury themselves, seeking to humble themselves as absolutely and as permanently as possible, for exaltation comes only through humility—pushing past the throng, the monks stormed to Golgotha and calling their brethren forward, to the great astonishment and fear of the weary, began erecting an enormous cross on the very site where it was believed Christ himself was crucified.

As the structure reached full tilt and was secured, the lead monk raised his arms in the air and addressed the crowd that had gathered at the site, calling out to them with incandescent pathos, his eyes aflame, his hands like swords cutting thin, dry, scaly bracts. "O heathens, harlots, and heretics, O ye of little faith, you have let yourselves be deceived by a trickster! You have fallen prey to temptations and to ruses! To the calling not of the spirit but of the flesh! An evil one is amongst you, juggling your souls with terrible facility as if they were but shiny baubles. Know this: He who claimed to be He was not He. The abdication is a gross falsehood! Do you believe that the crucifixion can be undone? Do you believe that salvation is not eternal? Do you believe that the Lord your God would forsake you? O, how I mourn and weep for you! How the Prophet mourns and weeps! You have exacerbated the wounds of the Man of Sorrows. You have crucified him anew a thousand times. You have salted the stigmata! But the final hour has not yet come; the Day of Judgment has not yet passed; the moment remains for you to repent. The End of Time cannot be brought to an end; the clock cannot be kept from stopping. Fear! Fear! Fear! For the Lord is coming, and the hour will be fierce. Remember the words of Jeremiah: ,Hear this now, O foolish people, without understanding, who have eyes and see not, and who have ears and hear not: ,Do you not fear Me?' says the Lord. ,Will you not tremble at My presence, who have placed the sand as the bound of the sea, by a perpetual decree, that it cannot pass beyond it? And though its waves toss to and fro, yet they cannot prevail; though they roar, yet they cannot pass over it. But this people has a defiant and rebellious heart; they have revolted and departed. They do not say in their heart, ,Let us now fear the Lord our God.'" And he continued quoting Jeremiah, fulminating with brio and gleeful wrath: "Your own wickedness will correct you, and your backslidings will rebuke you. Know therefore and see that it is an evil and bitter thing that you have forsaken the Lord your God. ,The fear of God is not in you,' says the Lord God of hosts, ,The fear of God is not in you!' Be wretched and mourn and weep. Let your laughter be turned to mourning and your joy to gloom.' Gather before the cross, prostrate yourselves in humility, reject the heathen trickster and return to your

God! In the dark dark night, the Christ revealed himself to me and said to build a cross, for he is to return to die for you again, and he was full of weeping for you, he cried tears of blood, nearly drowning me in his sorrow. He cried bitter tears of gall and blood—Repent now! The time is nigh! O heathens and heretics, save yourselves now!"

While many fell to their knees in horror, some lashing themselves with crops, others whipping themselves with sticks, others cutting themselves with glass, others grinding stones against their flesh, there were scores of people who ridiculed and mocked the monks, rejecting their visions as hallucinations and projections, as their refusal to recognize the apostasy of the very Son of God and they laughed at the monks and the penitent ones, denying salvation and the cross, denying Judgment Day, denying the end of time, and they began to dance around the monks and the renewed believers chanting: Amor solum! Amor solum! Amor solum! as they threw dirt at them, but when they attempted to tear the monks' clothes off and tickle them, the lead monk cut through the jests and the laughter and seizing one of the revelers, struck him across the face,

then knocked him to the ground with his staff and holding him beneath it, fumed, "As the crackling of thorns under a pot, so is the laughter of the fools! Woe unto you that are full! for ye shall hunger. Woe unto you that laugh now! for ye shall mourn and weep."

When another reveler came at the monk, the other monks attacked him and thrust him to the ground, too, holding the culprit under their staffs, watching as he squirmed beneath their might, watching as he winced with their every kick, watching as he squinted as they spit at him. "Be not like these lost ones, people, repent! They are like chaff that the wind blows away, and the Lord laughs at the wicked, for He sees that their day is coming!"

As the monk ground the staff into the reveler's chest and quashed his feet, the weapon lighting against his body with force, more and more people gathered before the spectacle, even a swarm of Jews, and as he gazed at them, the monk suddenly related his complete vision, asserting that the earthquake was not the work of Triboulet, who falsely claimed ownership of the act in order to deceive the multitude, but that it was the work of God. "Draw you nigh Jew, for the time is at hand, draw you nigh one and all. In the cleaving of this land there is the work of the Lord. The earthquakes that we suffered were not the work of man. Listen! Ye who have ears to hear, hear! The promises that the prophets of Israel said the Messiah was appointed to fulfill but never did are now at hand—through the cleaving of this land, there will be unification. The works of the Lord are strange and incomprehensible, paradoxes too extraordinary for us to understand. I was afflicted by them, too, but the Lord instructed me in His plan. Listen! What gave rise to woes and tribulations should have given rise to joy. The Lord has broken apart the land to unite; the Lord has divided in order to assemble. Jew, the Christ has come to finally deliver you from the oppression of the Gentile enemies; through destruction, he has sought to bring together those scattered in the Diaspora. Listen, Jew: — it was revealed to me that He is coming to at last restore the Davidic Kingdom and to establish peace, but this can only be achieved through war. A new covenant is to be announced. The Lord is strange; do not question his ways. The time is

upon us as never before; the ancient promises for land, nationhood, kingship, and blessing are to finally be fulfilled—the political powers shall be defeated! The time is nigh; the hour has truly come—repent!"

The Jews were astonished by these proclamations, and as the monks continued to beat the revelers, the Jews cast their hats away, removed their garb, and wept with joy at the knowledge of the fulfillment of the prophecies of the prophets of Israel. Approaching the other monks, the Jews asked for their hair to be sheared and then to be baptized, for they wanted to return to their people anew and to share the Good News with them as Christians, to demonstrate through acts the transformation that was at hand. And as their hair was being cut and they were undergoing the baptismal ritual, the head monk organized the erection of two other crosses and once they were built, flanking the main cross on Golgotha, though not superseding nor excelling it in height, the revelers who had been crushed under foot were affixed to the crosses and all present believed that the end of time was near and that the world's final turn to eternal joy was soon to come.

HOLY WEEK

All in what was formerly Jerusalem gathered at Golgotha, including the restored believers, the converted Jews, those who still doubted but were astonished by the spectacle of the newly risen crosses as well as by the revelers hanging from the instruments of torture, which flanked the one and only true instrument, and the forlorn and dismayed devotees of Triboulet, who remained doubtful but were still despairing, wondering if he did perhaps descend into the center of the earth in order to detonate it, or if he was not in fact who he proclaimed to be. And as word of the return of the Christ quickly sped around the world, others began to journey to Golgotha, though there was little time to reach the site, but they tried nonetheless, for they thought that the end of the world was imminent and they wanted to directly witness the spectacle—there was even a mass conversion of a swarm of Muslims, and though many remained skeptical and did not abandon their faith, although astounded by the acts of their former congregants they were devastated by the news of both Triboulet and the head monk, for if Triboulet was who he professed to be, their religion was annulled once and for all, yet even if he was not and the true Christ was to return, it was still annulled, so that day, in the midst of their affliction, no Imam sounded the call to prayer and there was a quiet on earth as never before since, aside from the silenced minarets, while the revived believers wanted to rejoice through sounding church bells, there were none to sound, let alone churches in which to ring them, for the work of Triboulet and his troupe was so thorough and complete; nonetheless, the rejoicing of believers was heard throughout the city as they exulted over the coming of the Savior, though such news also should have filled them with terror, and the head monk found those who were purely joyous over the event naïve and superficial, and he was amused by the believers having rung scores and scores of tiny bells in lieu of real church bells—the irony of their resembling in tone a jester's foot bells was completely lost on them.

The Jews and Muslims who had not yet converted washed and shaved their heads in preparation for baptism and when the first crowing of the cock was heard, all trembled with anticipation, turning to one another almost in shock, for as much as they did believe that the actual true Christ was to return, the signaling fowl was a confirming fact that solidified their belief, made it not a belief but knowledge of something true. The monks then called out, asking God to "bless the palm branches," to make them "a protection to all places into which they would be brought," pleaded that God "expel with his right hand all adversity," that He "bless and protect all who dwell in them, who have been redeemed by the Lord Jesus Christ," and they spoke of the dove conveying the olive branch to Noah's ark and to the multitude, and there was a great and solemn rejoicing, and the people rang the bells again. The monks all sung in unison, *Collegerunt, Quid faciemus*, & *Unus autem ex ipsis*, then recited from memory passages from St. Matthew's Gospel, because no copies of the Bible could be found ... After their recitations, they again blessed the palms and olive branches, sprinkled them with holy water, censed them, and after one final prayer, distributed them amongst the people in the city, at which time the other monks began singing the *Pueri Hebraeorum* and the children of the former

Jerusalem spread their garments over the pathway and cried out, "Hosanna to the Son of David; Blessed is He that cometh in the name of the Lord," repeating their call continuously as Triboulet's minions stood at the furthest distance, watching them from afar with astonishment, their incredulity increasing as the procession began, with the monks and the people carrying the blessed palms as the choir sang the antiphons *Cum appropinquaret*, *Cum audisset*, and *Multa turba*, and then *Magno salutis*, a hymn that made many weep and fall to their knees in humility, though the sound of laughter was heard from afar, subtly penetrating if not disrupting the song of praise, which compelled the believers to quell the wicked noise as they faithed on, singing with greater and greater ardor. When they reached the threshold of the door to the Church of the Holy Sepulchre, the monks sang the *Domine miserere*, and the believers responded with the *Kýrie, eléison*, which they sang three times in all, each time envisioning their victory and the death of laughter, singing *altiori voce cantando*. As they crossed over the doorway, one of the monks began the responsory *Ingrediente Domino*, singing it entirely in organum, then leaving the church, they reentered the city singing it again, and as they retraced their steps to the Holy Sepulchre, they sang the *Civitatem istam* & the *Beatam me dicent* until they circled back to the church, where all stood silently before the monks, one of whom stepped forward to deliver a sermon of worth as they prepared for the final hour, compelling everyone to confess their sins, and a weeping and a wailing and a gnashing of teeth was heard as never before, with the believers castigating themselves for their loss of faith and their obeisance to the trickster—the monks were stern and mute, listening as the deferent ones mourned then at last rejoiced because of the mercy that they were being shown by the Lord, although the former Jews and Muslims did not castigate themselves as the others, but embraced one another as never before and in profound reverence, expressed their love for the actual one true God.

While the people remained in their contrite positions, the monks sang in unison, incanting the *Gloria, laus, et honor* & *Cui puerile decus*, with the penitent ones responding in return, repeating the verses as best they could as an elder monk avowed: the time is nigh, the ludic Sunday is upon us, prompting one of the former Jews to quickly correct the monk, saying "ludica Sunday," while the sound of laughter penetrated their celebration from afar once again, disturbing the former Jew, who thought he heard the monk laugh, too, that he was perhaps mocking him, but he wasn't sure, and as he gazed up at him, thought he saw him smirking as he raised his hand in thanks, repeating *ludica Sunday*, jangling his bells and making the sign of the cross over the former Jew, whose doubts over what the monk actually said were promptly quelled by a sudden great trumpeting, and those gathered at the site watched as the head monk came trotting to Golgotha from afar on the Arabo-Friesian, provoking the deduction that he had caught Triboulet, for he was riding the prankster's stately black horse, in tow, a donkey upon which a large sack was bound, the object squirming and twisting, groans issuing from it, cries, eerie bestial growls, and near-hysterical guffaws—they fantasized then about beating, whipping, and torturing the trickster, burning him at the stake for his transgressions and violent, sacrilegious crimes, malefactions so abominable that no punishment was at all apposite for them, save eternal condemnation in the deepest darkest circle of hell. And as the head monk came closer to Golgotha, all shouted, screamed, and cursed, their gestures making them into an animated grotesque tableaux, or medieval woodcuts come to life as they foamed and fumed at the mouth, condemning Triboulet and his troupe, warning them that "the day and the hour is near," that there was "still time," that they "could repent," that "redemption" remained possible "even for heretics" as "wicked and evil" as they, and one of the more inflamed believers fulminated, waving his arms in the air like violent flags, stuttering, spitting words from between his teeth like bullets sizzling from the radiant muzzle of a Gatling gun:

"Ƒ-f-f-faith offerſ—uſ—much ... m-m-m-more, ſomething much ... ſt-ſt-ſt-ſtron-ger; thankſ to ... ſ-ſ-ſ-ſal-va-va-va-tion, q-q-quite-other-joyſ ... are at our-c-c-c-com-m-m-mand; inſtead of athletes and—abſurd—conteſts and frivolous ſports, inſtead of—ſ-ſ-ſ-ſ-ſexual—licenſe and ... f-f-f-flee-ting pleaſures, wwwe have our—m-m-m-mar-tyrſ—the athletes of the ſp-ſp-ſp-ſpir-it! En-g-g-g-gage in that conteſt and ſ-ſ-ſee who winſ! And if wwwe—want blood, we will—have it, yet it will not ſ-ſ-ſim-ply-be-the blood of the b-b-b-bat-tle-field, b-b-b-but ... the ſa-cred—blood—of the C-C-C-Chriſt ... endowing uſ with eternal life, and the-blood—of your f-f-f-flayed bah-bah-bah-bah-dieſ-periſhing—in the f-f-f-flames ... of righteouſneſs! Where will your ſtrength be then? Where your kineticiſm? Where your wondrous leaping? Where your ſtupid f-f-f-fleet-ing-or-ga-ga-ga-ga-ga-ga-ga-gaſmſ? Think what awaitſ uſ n-n-n-now, think ... of hiſ-t-t-t-triumph! There are yet other ſ-ſ-ſ-ſpec-ta-ta-ta-cleſ:

that f-f-f-final ... and everlaſt-
ing—Day—of Judgment, that d-
d-d-day that waſ not ex-pec-ted
and waſ even l-l-l-l-l-l-laughed
at b-b-by Tri-bou-let and hiſ t-
t-t-t-trrrroupe, b-b-b-but—the
whole old world and all it gave
b-b-b-birth—to are t-t-to be c-c-
c-con-ſumed in one—holy—c-c-
c-con-f-f-f-flag-g-g-g-gggration.
When your j-j-j-jeſter and hiſ a-
b-b-b-bom-inable ... minionſ will
b-b-b-be devoured! When h-h-h-
holineſſ will—tear—the ſ-ſ-ſ-ſin-
ew from—out—your fleſh, ſt-ſt-
ſt-rip-ping it from your very-
boneſ! What an ample breadth
of ſightſ there will b-b-b-be then!
At which we ſhall g-g-g-gaze
in—wonder! At which we ſh-ſh-
ſh-ſhall ... l-l-l-laugh! At which
re-j-j-j-joice! At which ex-ult!
For wwwe will ſee m-m-m-many
great kingſ who were p-p-p-pro-
claimed to have been taken up into heaven, groaning in the deep-
eſt darkneſſ together with thoſe
who c-c-c-claimed to have—wit-
neſſed ... th-th-th-their ap-p-p-p-
po-the-o-ſſſ-ſiſ and their freedom
from G-G-God through ... Tri-
bou-let! Dark—energy? Dark m-
m-m-m-mmat-ter? What of the
da-da-dark-neſſ ... of the inferno, O you p-p-p-pri-mate wor-
ſhipping aſſeſ! When wwwe ſee
thoſe wiſe ... philoſopherſ who
perſuaded their d-d-d-diſcipleſ

that—nothing—waſ of any concern to G-G-G-God and who
affirmed to them either that we
have no ſoulſ or that our ſ-ſ-ſ-
ſoulſ—will not re-turn to their
... original b-b-b-bah-dieſ! Now
they will be aſhamed b-b-be-fore
thoſe d-d-d-ſcipleſ, aſ they will
be b-b-b-burned together with
them! Beati in regno c-c-c-coe-
leſ-ti, vvvvvvi-de-bunt ppppp-
po-enas d-d-d-dam-na-t-t-t-tor-
um, ut bb-b-b-b-beatitudo—illiſ
... m-m-m-magis ... c-c-c-compla-
cent! Nature! Ha! What ſortſ
of thingſ are thoſe which the
eye haſ not ſeen n-n-nor th-th-
th ear heard, and which have
n-n-n-not come in-to the—hu-
hu-hu-man—heart? They are
more ppp-plea-ſing than the cir-
cuſ and the c-c-c-com-ic and t-
t-t-tra-gic—ſtageſ and wreſtling
ringſ and gameſ of j-j-j-jeſterſ
... and their evil ilk! Take your
rockſ, take your g-g-g-ge-ol-ogy,
take your ſ-ſ-ſ-ſ-ſ-ſci-enceſ, and—
ſtand—with them in your de-de-
de-ſertſ! What do you baſe ...
pppp-po-ſi-ti-viſtſ k-k-k-know—of
life?! Ab-b-b-b-bom-i-na-tion
of A-b-b-b-bom-i-nationſ!
We t-t-t-take the b-b-b-blood
of the Lord, of the Sav-ior J-
J-J-J-Je-ſuſ C-C-C-Ch-riſt,
and—ſtand—in—etttttttter-ni-ty
f-f-f-for all of t-t-t-time aſ you
de-de-de-ſcend in the ... f-f-f-

flameſ and f-f-f-fire and p-p-p-
pitch—of the in-f-f-f-erno—with
your v-v-v-vul-gar B-B-B-
Bau-boſ and your v-v-v-voodle
em-b-b-b-brace-of ... m-m-m-
m-matter! The w-w-w-world
iſ n-n-n-not a ca-ca-car-nival;
life iſ not a ... ga-ga-ga-game!
A-b-b-b-b-b-bom-i-nation of

De-de-de-ſo-lation! Repent,
or ... b-b-b-burn—forever in
the f-f-f-fireſ of e-ter-nal da-
da-da-dam-nation! The t-t-t-
tentſ of the un-go-go-go-god-ly
ſhall b-b-b-be t-t-t-torn—down!
Forever ... b-b-b-burn, ...
b-b-b-burn, b-b-b-burn!"

Drawing the horse to a full ſtop as the man finished his ſtut-
tering rant, the head monk then raised the animal's front legs
high into the air, pulling back on the reins and shouting something that sounded like THUNDER DOWN, though many
weren't sure exactly what he said, but after he dismounted
the horse, he gripped the rope tight in his hands and yanked
the large sack from the donkey to the earth, dragging the
body with such force that the animal was also pulled to the
ground, wincing and shrieking as if it too was being killed.
Once all of the believers gathered round the groaning entity,
the monks handed each of them whips and everyone inſtantly
began ſtriking the body, raising their weapons high in the air
and snapping them with incredible brio, one by one, slowly,
rhythmically, each following upon the other, each savoring
the other's blow, each relishing the muffled growling of the
entity as they beat it, the whips rising in the air and falling
down like fierce bolts of lightning, cracking againſt the body,
which twiſted and convulsed under the snaps of the leather,
its bound feet curling as if ſtruck with cattle prods, its head
jerking, twiſting, juddering, its torso lurching in the air as
the whips came down in swifter succession, no longer fluidly

but frantically, pummeling the entity, a chain of brutal weap-
onry striking with unrestrained ferocity, each of the torturers
throwing the weight of their entire body into the snapping
of their whips, driving the entity across the earth, some running up to kick, punch, or beat it directly, devoid of any me-
diating object, yearning as they did to feel the wounded flesh
of Triboulet pulse under their hands as they remorselessly
pounded his body, and as all of the spectators closed in on
the entity to pummel it directly, the monks came forward and
handed them knives and their eyes gleamed with malicious
delight as they seized the sharp blades and knelt before the
entity and slowly pushed the weapons into its body, for that
is all it was to them, an indistinct entity, but they watched
in terrible astonishment as no blood issued forth from the
form … Enraged, they stabbed the object with greater and
greater force, driving their knives into it as they shouted, "*die,
die, die,*" the misshapen form contorting under their devices,
though, still, no blood issued from it and they stood up in horror, for while the entity seemed not to contain any body fluids
at all, their knives appeared to be dripping with blood and as
they gazed at each other, believed that those before them were
saturated with blood, too. Coiling back, their hands seemed to
be stained red—motionless, as if time had ceased, they stood
still as the head monk addressed them, calling out: *How shall
you comfort yourselves, the murderers of all murderers? Who will
wipe that blood off of you? What water is there for you to clean
yourselves?* … and each of his questions struck them like blinding bolts of light, but they remained immobilized as the head
monk walked between them, bent down, then cut open the

burlap sack and began unwinding it, till at last he unfurled
the body, which tumbled and rolled over the earth, bumping
against rock and root, and each of them gazed at it in horror as
the monk drew away the fabric from the entity's head, kissed it
on the lips, and announced: *Where is God? I will tell you. You
have killed him—all of you are his murderers! What was holiest
and mightiest of all that the world has yet owned has bled to death
under your knives: who will wipe the blood off you? What water
is there for you to clean yourselves? What festivals of atonement,
what sacred games shall you have to invent? Is not the greatness
of this deed too great for you? It is, it is, but it is not too great for I,
it is not too great for those capable of becoming gods themselves! ...*
and reaching up, the head monk grabbed his scalp as if he was
going to tear it off, but it was not his hair and scalp that he was
rending, but a thin prosthetic mask as he said: *Cucullus non
facit monachum,* revealing that he was in fact Triboulet, not
at all a monk, and as the jester's fierce laughter cut through
the crowd and he rattled and rattled his bells and sounded
the *alalagē,* the believers were full of astonishment and dropped their knives, aghast at the scheme, convulsing with in-
conceivable terror for, what—*who* was it? Or: *what* was it—
what did they kill? *The true Christ?* Did Triboulet deceive
them into killing the actual King of Kings? Did they brutally
murder Him before He could be crucified again? Is it possible to kill a god? Why did the entity not bleed but saturate
them with blood? Was Triboulet the victorious master of
the world? As they pondered each question and the multitude of others that flurried through their brains as violently
as they plunged their knives into the body, they were further

discombobulated, almost thrust into vertigo by the sudden and raucous entrance of Aurora, who came charging in with the ship-car and all her attendants, the main troupe, the goats, monkeys, hyenas, and kids, who ran through the site with abandon, cackling without restraint, their gleeful noise echoing in the air as Triboulet and Aurora removed the revelers from the crosses to prepare for the final crucifixion and spectacle of spectacles as the cock made its second signal.

The believers stood over the body of the victim in gravid silence, overcome with unspeakable horror, for as they studied it, gazing at the figure's long hair, beard, and facial structure, they concluded that it was the Christ, some of them rearing back in terror, some fainting, others vomiting, enucleating themselves, or committing suicide, though one more formidable believer approached the god to gaze at Him—It?—in closer detail and when he knelt before the deity, he placed his hand on its head and caressed its hair, a tear falling from his eye onto its face; as he began convulsing with sorrow, he felt the body of the deity stir beneath his touch. Startled, he recoiled in horror, disturbed that he was actually face to face with the living Christ, a god that he participated in mutilating, and as he fell backwards in astonishment, he heard it whisper something, but could not make out the utterance and so he approached the deity, slowly stepping towards it, full of trepidation and fear, his body shuddering as he knelt over it again: hovering there, he felt the hand of it reach out and touch him—it drew his ear close to its lips and communicated something to him, but he was not sure if the god actually spoke, or if he heard the ſtatement echoing within his soul, but upon receiving the terrible revelation he collapsed:

"Ceci n'eſt pas un Chriſt; il était un simulacra."

As two of the troupe members seized the body and lifted it off the ground, Triboulet barked to the people like a carney, blowing upon his three horns, enticing one and all into witnessing the greateſt attraction on earth, the ſpectacle of ſpectacles and sacrifice of sacrifices, an event unparalleled in history, a ritual that could perhaps even undo creation itself.

The appointed time is near! When it comes, what will you say? Would it be better if I had never returned, or will my returning be seen as the grandeſt and moſt unexpected repetition of all, the act which gives man back to man as never before? Come one, come all! Gaze upon the figure we hold before you, gaze upon *God the Father himself* ...

And to the raucous uproar of the troupe, which sounded every single inſtrument in its arsenal, and the uproarious din of the kids, and the frolicsome noises of the animals, the naked body of the deity was diſplayed to the crowd, and save for the fact that he had a beard and long hair, he resembled Triboulet exactly, was identical to him in height, weight, and contour, but as all gazed at his body in bewilderment, they noticed that deſpite his having been furiously whipped and ſtabbed, it contained no bruises. When the troupe members brought the indiſtinct entity before Aurora, she asked him:

Are you the deity who claims to be the only deity? ... but the figure remained silent, and Aurora was greatly astonished and questioned him again: Are you not the one who said, 'Thou shalt have no other gods before me ... for I the Lord thy God am a jealous God'? and again he did not answer, but when prompted once more with the same question, though no one saw his lips move, all heard a terrible voice resounding in the air, and this is what it said: "I suffer not a woman to teach, nor to usurp authority over the man, but to be in silence. It is not permitted unto them to speak; but they are commanded to be under obedience, as also saith the law."

When the portentous pronouncement finally ceased, Aurora and the other women jangled their foot bells and burst into guffaws, as did the members of the troupe, who were accompanied by the kids, monkeys, midgets, and hyenas, but no laughter was as exalted and resonant as that of the numerous other elegant figures present amongst them, who laughed and rocked on their chairs and shouted: Is just this not Godliness, that there are Gods, but no God? and their laughter did not cease, but continued and continued until they laughed themselves to death, enjoying a good and joyful end as the women pelted the naked god with salted ribs and Triboulet implored: If a shrine is to be set up, *a shrine has to be destroyed*: that is the law! *Patere legem, quam ipse tulisti!* so when Aurora asked the crowd: What am I to do with this wrath-beard of a God who claims to be the only God? ... With one voice they answered, "Crucify him!" to which Aurora rejoined: That is not our way, but each must perish by the law that they establish, so—thus shall it be!

Then the midgets threw God to the ground and called out: What color robe should be put on him? And one shouted: *Scarlet!* but another protested, arguing: In Mark the son was dressed in a purple robe, while another said: Luke didn't remember the color but said that the robe was gorgeous, and someone else shouted back: It wasn't a robe; it was a cloak, to which the soldiers responded: Let's put him in a gorgeous scarlet cloak with a purple belt.

And so it was decided, and Aurora and the aged women dressed the malefactor, and plaiting a crown of banana branches, they placed it on his head, and a stick in his right hand. Falling on their knees before him they jeered at him: 'Hail, the one and only God!' They laughed at him, and pelted him with bananas.

When the crowd finished mocking him, Aurora and the aged women stripped off the robe, the midgets and the kids leapt upon the figure and knocked it to the ground and took handfuls of soil and rubbed it on his chest, shoulders, face, back, and buttocks, and they even took handfuls of the moist earth and rubbed it over his genitals and chanted: *Amor solum! Amor solum! Amor solum!* Then he was led away to be crucified and when they reached the instrument of instruments, they offered him a drink of honey mixed with water; after tasting it he asked for more, because it was so satisfying, and as he drank and drank from Aurora's cup, several of the enormous bells from Kent Cathedral were wheeled into the site; once in place, they were clanged so frantically it created a terrible din, with all gazing in astonishment as the figure was lifted in the air and placed upon the cross, but they weren't sure whether to hammer him in place with three, four, or four-teen nails. Since they enjoyed banging things so much, they decided to use fourteen and to make the hammering of the nails into a song, and so it was, and they beat the nails into his body, affixing him to the cross, each hammering of the nail amplified by the thundering beat of a hundred timpani sound-ing in unison: boom, boom, boom, and another nail: boom, boom, boom, and another nail: boom, boom, boom, the ring-ers joining in with the pull of the bells, the women joining in with the shriek of the *ololugē*, the midgets joining in with their high pitched shrills, the kids joining in with their frenzied cackling, the animals with their natural array of sounds, but with each nail driven into the figure's body, no blood issued forth, and as the final nail was driven in, every instrument was sounded: bells, whistles, percussion, brass, all erupting with the full force of their bodies as they watched the figure writhe upon the cross, thrashing about like a fish in a net as Triboulet hammered a sign above his head:

Ceci n'est pas un Dieu

The figure, turning from right to left, noticed that the crosses on either side of him were empty as the third crowing of the fowl cut through the air, but it was only an automaton.

The passers-by wagged their heads and laughed at the god, chuckling:

So you are the one who mistakes retribution for justice!

He thinks that eternal love created the inferno!

He believes that he is the only one—did he not see the other gods die from laughter? How ungodly you are!

If you wanted us to be nothing but pure spirit, why did you give us flesh—did you botch your creation and leave it to us to reconcile?!

You condemned the body, but what do those who have no desires know of bodies? What do those who have no bodies know of bodies!

He can create entire worlds, an earth, heaven, and hell, but he fears the voice of women!

What are you but a *folie circulaire!*

Even the kids, who knew not of such complexities, found him ridiculous and laughed at him, giggling freely and rattling their foot bells in the air.

From midnight an incandescent light suffused the whole land, which lasted until three in the morning; and about three the figure cried aloud, "*Lama sabachthani*," to which one of the midgets barked: All the world's a circus, but you're a crooked carney, and another midget added: He's runnin' a tent show scam! while yet one more shouted: Get your ass off the midway, boy, if you wanna see the mornin' light! but after another urged: Let's catch a storm and burn this mother's circus down—turn about! Triboulet called out: We have not forsaken you—we have *sacrificed* you out of necessity! For cleanliness's sake! To end the need for redemption once and for all—there is no renovation, only release into the flow of time! That is what all must reconcile themselves to. The end of the End has come! I am he who you thought was He but I am no longer He! *Ecce enim cosmos intra vos est!*

Aurora ran at once and fetched a sponge, which she soaked in mead and held to the entity's lips on the end of a stick, and he sucked on the sponge, drawing all of the liquid out of it, for he was insatiable.

The figure again cried aloud and breathed his last. At that moment, Triboulet turned to all and after sounding a note on his three horns, he exulted:

With no blood, there is no debt. With no God, there is no law. It is finished! *God is dead!*

Instantly, the curtain of the temple was torn in two from top to bottom. The earth shook, rocks split, and the circles of the inferno were each broken and destroyed, releasing at last all of the pagan artists and scientists from below.

Behold the Earth—we are autochthons! The *turnabout* has come, not the thunder down! The promise of the gospels has now been annulled, the evangelum broken. Truly I tell you: the present generation has lived to see it all. Heaven has passed away, God has died, and the inferno & the purgatorio have been eliminated. May the words once spoken in my name now and forever pass away, too. Go ye therefore, and release all nations, freeing them *in nomine Agonism, et Risus, & Funambulatorum Artes.* Moses, Christ, Mohammed or—Scurra!

9

Ecce Homo ? Ecce Humus! Ecce Cosmos! Ecce Bălatro!

0

Standing at the base of Golgotha, Triboulet raised a sledge-hammer over his head and all watched in complete silence as he brought the tool down hard upon the infamous rock, a strike echoed by a thunderous battery of timpani, and he struck and struck again and again and after the fifth strike, the rock split in half, the cross upon which God was affixed tumbled backwards, and a parliament of owls issued forth from the place that formerly housed the rock, each soaring in a different direction, perching upon trees, buildings, and elsewhere, Triboulet tracing their pathways, watching them cut through the sky with joy, one of them landing on his shoulder and stretching out its wings and turning its head round and round.

In hoc signo vinces! The sign of victory has come—the Chi Rho has broken; the earth has split; the sea has changed; cosmos is chaos ~

א בְּרֵאשִׁית בָּרָא אֱלֹהִים, אֵת הַשָּׁמַיִם, וְאֵת הָאָרֶץ

ב וְהָאָרֶץ, הָיְתָה תֹהוּ וָבֹהוּ, וְחֹשֶׁךְ, עַל-פְּנֵי תְהוֹם; וְרוּחַ אֱלֹהִים, מְרַחֶפֶת עַל-פְּנֵי הַמָּיִם

ג וַיֹּאמֶר אֱלֹהִים, יְהִי אוֹר; וַיְהִי-אוֹר

ד וַיַּרְא אֱלֹהִים אֶת-הָאוֹר, כִּי-טוֹב; וַיַּבְדֵּל אֱלֹהִים, בֵּין הָאוֹר וּבֵין הַחֹשֶׁךְ

ה וַיִּקְרָא אֱלֹהִים לָאוֹר יוֹם, וְלַחֹשֶׁךְ קָרָא לָיְלָה; וַיְהִי-עֶרֶב וַיְהִי-בֹקֶר, יוֹם אֶחָד

ו וַיֹּאמֶר אֱלֹהִים, יְהִי רָקִיעַ בְּתוֹךְ הַמָּיִם, וִיהִי מַבְדִּיל, בֵּין מַיִם לָמָיִם

ז וַיַּעַשׂ אֱלֹהִים, אֶת-הָרָקִיעַ, וַיַּבְדֵּל בֵּין הַמַּיִם אֲשֶׁר מִתַּחַת לָרָקִיעַ, וּבֵין הַמַּיִם אֲשֶׁר מֵעַל לָרָקִיעַ; וַיְהִי-כֵן

ח וַיִּקְרָא אֱלֹהִים לָרָקִיעַ, שָׁמָיִם; וַיְהִי-עֶרֶב וַיְהִי-בֹקֶר, יוֹם שֵׁנִי

ט וַיֹּאמֶר אֱלֹהִים, יִקָּווּ הַמַּיִם מִתַּחַת הַשָּׁמַיִם אֶל-מָקוֹם אֶחָד, וְתֵרָאֶה, הַיַּבָּשָׁה; וַיְהִי-כֵן

כ וַיֹּאמֶר אֱלֹהִים--יִשְׁרְצוּ הַמַּיִם, שֶׁרֶץ נֶפֶשׁ חַיָּה; וְעוֹף יְעוֹפֵף עַל-הָאָרֶץ, עַל-פְּנֵי רְקִיעַ הַשָּׁמָיִם

¹ Ἀποκάλυψις Ἰησοῦ Χριστοῦ· ἣν ἔδωκεν αὐτῷ ὁ θεός, δεῖξαι τοῖς δούλοις αὐτοῦ ἃ δεῖ γενέσθαι ἐν τάχει, καὶ ἐσήμανεν ἀποστείλας διὰ τοῦ ἀγγέλου αὐτοῦ τῷ δούλῳ αὐτοῦ Ἰωάννῃ, ² ὃς ἐμαρτύρησεν τὸν λόγον τοῦ θεοῦ καὶ τὴν μαρτυρίαν Ἰησοῦ Χριστοῦ, ὅσα εἶδεν. ³ μακάριος ὁ ἀναγινώσκων καὶ οἱ ἀκούοντες τοὺς λόγους τῆς προφητείας, ὁ γὰρ καιρὸς ἐγγύς. ⁴ Ἰωάννης ταῖς ἑπτὰ ἐκκλησίαις ταῖς ἐν τῇ Ἀσίᾳ· χάρις ὑμῖν καὶ εἰρήνη ἀπὸ ὁ ὢν καὶ ὁ ἦν καὶ ὁ ἐρχόμενος καὶ ἀπὸ τῶν ἑπτὰ πνευμάτων ἃ ἐνώπιον τοῦ θρόνου αὐτοῦ, ⁵ καὶ ἀπὸ Ἰησοῦ Χριστοῦ, ὁ μάρτυς ὁ πιστός, ὁ πρωτότοκος τῶν νεκρῶν καὶ ὁ ἄρχων τῶν βασιλέων τῆς γῆς. Τῷ ἀγαπῶντι ἡμᾶς καὶ λύσαντι ἡμᾶς ἐκ τῶν ἁμαρτιῶν ἡμῶν ἐν τῷ αἵματι αὐτοῦ, ⁶ καὶ ἐποίησεν ἡμᾶς βασιλείαν ἱερεῖς τῷ θεῷ καὶ πατρὶ αὐτοῦ, αὐτῷ ἡ δόξα καὶ τὸ κράτος

بسم

الله الرحمن الرحيم ۞ ذلك الكتاب لا ريب فيه

هدى للمتقين ۞ الذين يؤمنون بالغيب ويقيمون الصلوة

ومما رزقناهم ينفقون ۞ والذين يؤمنون بما أنزل

من قبلك وبالآخرة هم يوقنون ۞

وأولئك هم المفلحون ۞

لم تنذرهم لا يؤمنون ۞ غشوة

أبصارهم ... وبالله واليوم الآخر وما ... أولئك على هدى من ربهم

امنوا ... الله ... في ضلال ... عليهم ... ولقد أفسدوا ... أنذرتهم ...

ومن الناس من يقول ... يخادعون الله والذين

... في قلوبهم ... وإذا قيل لهم لا تفسدوا في الأرض ...

قل أعوذ برب الناس ۞ إنما كانوا يكذبون ۞

۞ ملك الناس ۞ ... الخناس ۞ ... مصلحون ۞

قل ۞ من شر الوسواس ... الناس ۞ إله

الناس ۞ في صدور الناس ۞ من الجنة والناس ۞ الذي

يوسوس ۞

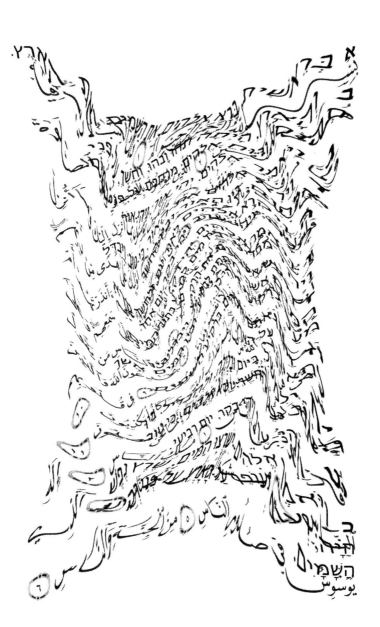

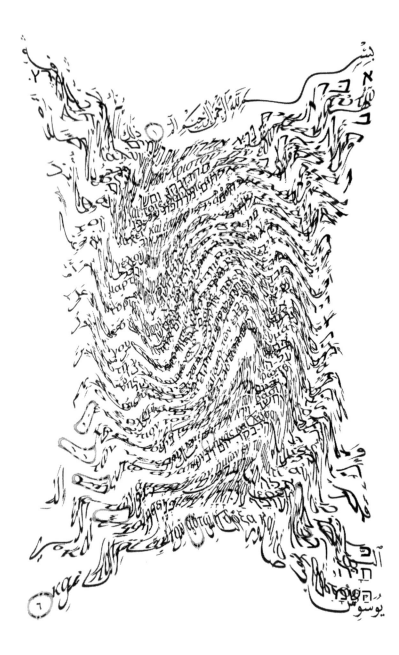

When the kids first began circling Circo Massenzio, it was with a degree of order and harmony, but as they continued circling it, they became more and more disordered, perhaps provoked by the wildly hot, almost violent temperature which, despite the fact that it was just here last spring, seemed to increase as they played, perhaps provoked by the strange geographical locale, or by sheer gr—

Over the next month, Aurora and the troupe leveled the ground where Golgotha once was and constructed a labyrinth on the site: the place was named anew Piazza Risus and all of the street signs and maps formerly denoting the former capital of Israel as Jerusalem had been passed to Bend Seeloraux City, and it was rife with goats and—

Listen: I sit on no glorious throne; I possess no crown; I have come only to clear the air, but as *we* stand before chaos at this moment, let us recognize that there will not be but sheep and goats—the world is split between those who oppose experimentation, for to them it is a violation of the 'law,' and those who uphold and pursue it, for they recognize no binding law, but only the task of continual overcoming! And so there are those who belong to the dead world, and those who belong to chaos, to the ever beckoning future upon which humanity is to test itself! The boundary lines of space and time must be reconceived—the higher history has begun! As never before, we are but undetermined animals, part human, part beast, no better than any creature on earth, nothing but cosmic dust. The time has come to reshape chaos! The time has come for *bōmolokhia*! For great *Tribouletions*!

And all rattled their foot bells, vigorously jingling them in the air.

After Triboulet and Aurora removed the dead god from the instrument of torture and placed him and each of the crosses in a pile on the left side of what was formerly Golgotha, they gathered the bodies of the elegant figures and brought them to the same spot as the troupe constructed one enormous funeral pyre of dried banana branches. Once it was complete, they placed the bodies on the pyre, then set it aflame, the fire burning with such intensity that it almost seemed like day, save for the brilliant stars glistening in the inky black sky and as the bodies burned, there was dancing and celebration, a general festive impertinence, with the musicians driving everyone into a complete frenzy, the beats and rhythms varying and

I

escalating in tandem with the fire, their bodies becoming looser and looser, more fluid, elastic, and dynamic, and they wove
into one another during their orgiastic rite like the sea rushing
into grottoes, or rain seeping into the earth as the figures on
the pyre burned, the water of their bodies completely having
evaporated, then the soft-tissue, and as the temperatures rose
and the celebrants broke and crashed into one another, fusing like tectonic plates, pushing everything above them up and
out and forcing it to reform and reconfigure itself, the fluids
in the skulls of the burning figures vaporized, the pressure
inside them building and building, increasing to its absolute
limit, till at last the skulls each exploded, a sound that excited
the musicians, stimulating them to intensify the rhythms,
provoking the final ecstatic rendering of the celebrants, who
exploded like meteors crashing into planets as pieces of the
vaults of the skulls of the dead figures were flung far from
their bodies, which were at last reduced to nothing but grey
ash and bone fragments, and as the fires died down and the
celebrants watched the animals screwing wildly, the sun rose
upon the newly formed lands that Triboulet created, the first
sunrise of the new dawn, the first sunrise of the Anno Risus,
the first true sunrise since the fourth year of Olympiad 202,
and everyone gathered the ashes and bone fragments of the
cremated gods and carried them to one of the new rivers.

When they reached the bank of the river, the bone fragments were placed before Triboulet, who stared into his mortar as if into a vortex or some infinitely contracting horizon,
and he took the pestle and began turning about, whirling and
whirling in a circle, his right palm facing the earth, his left the

sky, pivoting on his right foot with perfect agility, each revolution increasing in intensity and velocity. With ceremonial finality, he began chanting, then made ever tighter and tighter revolutions as if to eliminate or close the very circle he had formed, until he ceased whirling, removed his black cloak, and revealed a resplendent burgundy costume, and, kneeling before the mortar, methodically crushed the mass of bone fragments until they were triturated and then sprinkled the ashes into the water, which absorbed them

0

As the river flowed on, the waters gently surging over the banks, the kids stripped Triboulet of his ceremonial costume and then washed him with soil and all chanted: *Amor solum! Amor solum! Amor solum!* as they carried him back to what was formerly Jerusalem. When they reached the site of the crucifixion, they threw Triboulet into the air and out of their momentum, he did a somersault and landed on his hands and walked around the piazza, flipping back and forth from his hands to his feet, then tumbling and rolling and performing many acrobatic coups, which excited the monkeys so much that they began leaping around just like Triboulet, and as they leapt from object to object and from tree to tree, the hyenas chased after them, all laughing in their own manner, all overcome with joy, all exultant, and as the kids joined in, adding to the humorous din, the laughter of each was no longer distinguishable: — it became one unified but diverse chorus of elated sounds, which increased in intensity and pitch, and everyone was infected by the sound and the musicians put their instruments to rest as they too were overcome by laughter, seized by it, and as Triboulet thought of how he emancipated himself from his last intoxicating urge to play the savior through impersonating the monk, and how he made the believers directly experience the death of God, his body trembled, and when the kids saw him giggling, they leapt on him and started tickling him madly, because they loved the sound of his laughter, for he laughed as no other human had ever laughed, and as they tickled and tickled him, he cried out: I have so much chaos in myself! and his body went into spasms as he laughed with ever more freedom, and he trembled and

trembled as the sensations coursed through his body, powerful
erotic sensations, for the laughter was so unusual and titillat-
ing that he began to orgasm and the almost terrifying sublime
pitch of his voice provoked the kids further and they tickled
him with greater and greater force till his entire body quiv-
ered and shook, rocking back and forth on the earth as they
surrounded him, each kid jumping over every other, pushing
his or her way through the fractal of kids till Triboulet was
no longer visible, only an ever expanding cluster of laughing,
giggling bodies, one coalescing with the other, the wondrous
raucous sound suffusing the site as kid tumbled over kid, their
high pitched laughter rising over Triboulet's, who between
his guffaws announced that the new world had at last begun,
that the epoch of *asbestos gelōs* was upon them, the epoch of
asbestos gelōs, and while the kids continued to tickle him, his
words were chanted by Aurora and the troupe, transmitted
from person to person to person, each voice conveying his utterance, which was sounded from the new lands to beyond,
as was the laughter, drifting through borders and boundaries,
crossing seas, oceans, and mountains, crossing even galactic
boundaries, and as Aurora gazed at the kids, she saw this luminous fiery light streaming through their bodies; when they
separated, she noticed that they were juggling the light, and as
it bounced from hand to hand to hand, it resembled to her a
dancing star, for its light was so blinding and magnificent, as
was the sight of the kids leaping about, tossing the object back
and forth, its luminosity illuminating their faces, and as they
tossed the object higher and higher into the air, it mesmerized
the owls, and the ululating birds circled the kids, soaring over

them in ever greater and greater arcs, carving the air as if they were sculptors, their clear, searching, lucid eyes surveying the expanse of geography ſtretching before them, terrain truly incognita, as unexplored as the 12 rivers, and gliding through the air, they suddenly dived to the earth and around and about the kids, each of them slowing their pace and landing on the shoulder of a different kid, ſtretching their wings out, gazing into the diſtance as the kids caſt the luminous objeƈt into the sky

Over the next month, Aurora and the troupe leveled the ground where Golgotha once was and conſtruƈted a labyrinth on the site; the place was named anew Piazza Risus and all of the ſtreet signs and maps formerly denoting the former capital of Israel as Jerusalem had been changed to read *Sceloglaux City*, and it was rife with goats, monkeys, and hyenas and over each gate to the city of the now nameless geographical locale was written

Asbeſtos Gelōs

RISUS RISUS RISUS

COLOPHON

THE ABDICATION was typeset in InDesign 5.0.
The text, page numbers, and brackets are set in *Adobe Jenson Pro*.
The titles are set in *Charlemagne*.
The columns in Blackletter are set in *Wilhelm Klingspor Schrift*.
The Arabic types for *"Chaos of Letters"* are courtesy of DecoType.

THE ABDICATION is published by Contra Mundum Press
and printed by Lightning Source, which has received Chain of
Custody certification from: The Forest Stewardship Council,
The Programme for the Endorsement of Forest Certification,
and The Sustainable Forestry Initiative.

CONTRA MUNDUM PRESS
NEW YORK

CONTRA MUNDUM PRESS

Contra Mundum Press is dedicated to the value and the indispensable importance of the individual voice.

Contra Mundum Press will be publishing titles from all the fields in which the genius of the age traditionally produces the most challenging and innovative work: poetry, novels, theatre, philosophy — including philosophy of science and of mathematics — criticism, and essays. Upcoming volumes include the first translation into English of Nietzsche's "Greek Music Drama," Miklós Szentkuthy's *St. Orpheus Breviary: vol. 1, Marginalia on Casanova*, W. J. Bate's *Negative Capability*, Elio Petri's *Writings on Cinema and Life*, and Louis Auguste Blanqui's *Eternity by the Stars*.
For the complete list of forthcoming publications, please visit our website. To be added to our mailing list, send your name and email address to: info@contramundum.net

Contra Mundum Press
P.O. Box 1326
New York, NY 10276
USA
http://contramundum.net

ABOUT THE AUTHOR

RAINER J. HANSHE

was born in Tehran, Iran, and raised in New York.
He is a writer.

CPSIA information can be obtained at www.ICGtesting.com
Printed in the USA
BVOW012355220512

290590BV00002B/1/P

The American
BUREAUCRACY

· · · · · · · · · · · · · ·

Nelson-Hall Series in Political Science

Consulting Editor: Samuel C. Patterson

The Ohio State University